The Journey

Andrea Bocelli
Recorded by Giorgio De Martino

TRILOGY CHRISTIAN PUBLISHERS

TUSTIN, CA

Trilogy Christian Publishers
A Wholly Owned Subsidary of Trinity Broadcasting Network
2442 Michelle Drive
Tustin, CA 92780

The Journey

Copyright © 2023 by Andrea Boccelli

Original title: *In Cammino* by Andrea Bocelli © 2022 Mondadori Libri S.p.A.

Published by Mondadori Libri for the imprint Sperling & Kupfer.

Translator: Maeve Sullivan

No part of this book may be reproduced, stored in a retrieval system, or transmitted by any means without written permission from the author. All rights reserved. Printed in the USA.

Rights Department, 2442 Michelle Drive, Tustin, CA 92780.

Trilogy Christian Publishing/TBN and colophon are trademarks of Trinity Broadcasting Network.

For information about special discounts for bulk purchases, please contact Trilogy Christian Publishing.

Trilogy Disclaimer: The views and content expressed in this book are those of the author and may not necessarily reflect the views and doctrine of Trinity Christian Publishing or the Trinity Broadcasting Network.

10 9 8 7 6 5 4 3 2 1

Library of Congress Cataloging-in-Publication Data is available.

B-ISBN: 979-8-89041-758-9

E-ISBN: 979-8-89041-759-6

Dedication

Dear Father,

To you, Veronica, and everyone else who made this very special, courageous journey possible. I am here to say thank you. Thank you for this strong, solid endeavor, and this invitation to get back to the fundamental values of life.

It is easy to forget these values. Daily life can pull us all, both young and old, toward a superficiality that never comes to any good. But, most importantly, forgetting these values can be dangerous. My generation is most at risk of making this mistake, which can be much more serious than you might think. So, I strongly hope that my peers take this opportunity to listen carefully and embrace the ample food for thought before them.

Some pressing issues are too seldom debated. Treated as obsolete, they're outdated by the progress of this era's evolved societies. But the closer I get to adult life, the more I realize that they are far from obsolete. Faith, family, love, forgiveness, hope, prayer, and serenity—none of these can be bought or sold, and perhaps this is why they are very rarely discussed. Yet, they are the pillars of life.

I want to thank you, Father, for making me rediscover this beautiful word: *pilgrimage*. We are all like pilgrims facing a stretch of our journey every day. Those who have walked this road before us have left us with precious clues to a more virtuous path, along with food, light, and energy for the journey. Just think of the cathedrals erected throughout the centuries, the locations brimming with spirituality, the miracles carved in the memory of stone, the testimonies of the many voices who dedicated their entire existence to that light.

Holy is another word that has taken on a profoundly different meaning for me, thanks to this journey. What is and what is not holy? And, dear Father, I think I have learned that everything can be holy. Everything that is experienced with love, with the joy of a gift. Everything that chooses goodness. Just as you have always told me since I was a child.

Along the route from Saint Peter's Square to my grandparents' house in Lajatico, Italy, not only are the monasteries full of holiness but also the surrounding woods, valleys, and paths you rode through on horseback with Veronica, the grass you walked on, and the words and smiles you exchanged.

I would even say that all of life is holy. This pilgrimage has given me the courage to say that in earnest. And we need to hear it now more than ever. This is why I wanted to publicly thank you on behalf of those like me who strive and struggle to be a better person every day, one step at a time.

Matteo Bocelli

Contents

Introduction

The Reasons Behind Our Journey

This journey has been a dream of mine for a long time. A dream that became reality in spring 2021. A dream that took shape over 230 miles traveled on horseback. An intense, complex, exciting experience with plenty of setbacks but packed with extraordinary surprises.

A pilgrimage that my wife and I envisioned as a form of prayer expressed through discipline and physical effort, music, and encounters with others.

The Via Francigena itinerary embodies the desire of pilgrims from all over Europe to pray before the tomb of Peter the Apostle. It stretches over one thousand miles and is dotted with holy places, one-thousand-year-old testimonies of faith soaked into stone, dazzlingly beautiful works of art, and landscapes that make you wonder about creation and its Creator.

Crossing through five different countries and hundreds of towns, the Via Francigena is also a powerful conductor of culture. It is a meeting point, the nomadic home of a community that mingles throughout a sweeping space, under the warmth of the sun, beneath the nave of a church, inside the walls of a convent or in little villages.

It is a wonderful rambling trail through meadows and forests where you come upon intrepid people. Not content with the easy paradigms of materialism, these people are searching within, spurred by their sharp sense of adventure, ready to question their belief systems and marvel at what they find. As someone once said, the world of spirituality is for the brave.

Our journey was spiritual and yet so solid and concrete, with showers of rain and branches scratching our faces. It started out from the hub of Christianity, the tomb of Saint Peter, and ended on the rolling hills of Tuscany, where my family has lived for generations and where I myself was born and raised. So it was an inverted journey, not from my home to Rome but from Rome back home.

Full of excitement, we kicked off our expedition under the protection of a prayer by a great man of God, a pilgrim on Earth. The Holy Father himself, Pope Francis, came out to bless us on our journey.

The aim of a pilgrimage is usually to strengthen the traveler's faith. In our case, faith was already there, the cornerstone of our souls. Armed with this certainty, we embarked from the world's smallest state that spiritually embraces all other states: the Vatican. After that, heading out from Rome with its grandeur and boisterous beauty, we took on our journey in reverse, toward Tuscany, toward Valdera, toward my roots.

In my personal interpretation of existence, the direction of life inevitably points to a return to the father's home. Each individual can name this divine parent as they see fit. Even the lay philosopher Arthur Schopenhauer reckoned with an entity from which everything originates and to which everything returns. Referring to nature, he wrote that it is completely detached from the destiny of individuals. Because when their children fall, they fall back to the womb from which they are born; basically, a maternal figure awaiting the return of her children. We just need some humility and optimism to allocate a parent to nature itself. Then the human perspective is instantly transformed: from desperation to hope to faith.

So, Veronica and I set out on our pilgrimage with our fully fledged certainty of a heavenly father whose voice echoes in so many miracles and whose finger always points to the right path. The memory of this journey will remain with us forever throughout the rest of this greatest pilgrimage of ours.

Returning Home

Home and family have absolute priority in my heart. They are branded there with fire. This immense bond stems mostly from my childhood. To get me an education suited to my condition, my parents had to make the brave yet painful decision to send me to boarding school (with them being the ones who suffered the most).

During my crucial formative years, I lived away at school, stolen from my carefree life, compelled to grow up quickly, to experience forced autonomy. When a child is dragged into an alien environment at just six years old, brought to a far-off, rundown boarding school devoid of all comforts (I remember being made to wash my face and neck with freezing water every day and having squatting toilets), their mind melds the idea of home with the idea of maternal love and a father's emotional and protective aura. It becomes the truest and perfect depiction of heaven.

This left its mark on me even though I did not end up a homebody as an adult. Yet, temperamentally, I would be similar to German philosopher Immanuel Kant. He apparently used to leave his house for a walk at the same time every day. He was so precise that his neighbors supposedly synchronized their watches to his movements. Instead, destiny has given me a wandering life for the past thirty years.

When I was a child, my family's large farmhouse at La Sterza in Lajatico was always at the forefront of my mind and my sentimental thoughts. My moments of greatest joy were when my parents would come to the boarding house to get me for the Christmas or summer holidays. The birth of my children is possibly the only thing that could compare with that state of happiness. It was far greater than any other joyful moment of my life. Winning Sanremo Music Festival song contest, debuting at the Metropolitan, getting my university degrees (both honorary and earned)—none of these even came close.

My mother would also be impatient to have me home again. She told me she used to look out the window every morning to see how much the grain had grown. Once it was ready, she knew it was time for me to come home.

My summer holidays were an endless joy. The courtyard of our home would become the general headquarters of the dozen or so children who lived in the area. My grandmother Andreina would keep a watchful eye on us and get snacks for everyone. We formed gangs. We assigned ranks, from general to ordinary soldier. We played soccer. We made forays into fields and rivers, armed with slingshots—pure joy.

The Perfect Companion

I must admit that there was an ulterior motive for my pilgrimage along the Via Francigena. That strong, deep-rooted motive sprang from my passion for horses, not as a means of transport but as traveling companions.

The idea of making our pilgrimage on horseback was instinctive. I have always considered horses a means of freedom, perfect partners for true contact with nature.

The origin of this passion also dates back to my early years and my difficult time in boarding school. My grandfather Alcide wanted to buy me a horse for my eighth birthday. Sadly, he did not get the chance. He died just before my birthday. So my father took on that promise and bought me my first little horse, Stella, an Avelignese cross between eastern stallions and brood mares from Avelengo, Italy.

I remember how ecstatically happy I was that day. I was already in seventh heaven just for being back home. Then, to top it off, my mother and father brought me to Poggioncino, Italy, (where I still keep my horses to this day). We went into the stall, and they showed me the surprise. I was out of my mind with happiness. From then on, my thoughts and desires would always be there, alongside my little horse, Stella, who also had an excellent disposition. That experience shaped a passion that I still nurture to this day. Then I asked my father for a larger horse when I became a teenager. After doing his best to resist, he finally caved in and bought me Andris, a mare as black as tar.

In addition to being my favorite sport in my younger years, horseback riding has always been a privileged means of transport for me. Horses were my bicycle, my moped. I always broke them in myself, even as a little boy. My inexperience sometimes led to my being thrown off the horses, but I was stubborn and got the better of them each time in the end. I would always achieve what I had set in my sights.

I respect horses for their intelligence, their ability to show affection, their strong-willed nature, their athleticism, and the camaraderie you establish when you ride them. In my opinion, the perfect type of equestrian sport is "eventing," especially cross-country, a challenging discipline on both a sporting and technical level. Given my background, horseback riding has always been an equestrian sport for me. I consider cross-country to be horseback riding at its best. It has extremely appealing athletic implications along with practical functions.

You inevitably establish an intense relationship with your horse. For instance, I remember one extraordinary animal, an Arabian horse named Giasir that I loved dearly. He was a friend in a way. When he died, I was so upset I wrote a poem in his memory.

I brought some of my best horses on the journey from Rome to Lajatico, wonderful Andalusian horses trained for great exertion but not exactly suited to a route that is often rough and perilous. To make sure the journey did not become too risky— for the riders and, above all, for the horses—we brought along our friend and horse keeper Emiliano Cioni, the supreme protector of the Bocelli ranch. If the world were divided into those who create problems and those who resolve them, Emiliano is certainly one of the latter. Not only does he resolve problems, he doesn't make it feel like they're a burden, and if he can help it, you won't even know about them. We also had with us our dear friend Pasquale Beretta, one of the world's greatest experts in horses, renowned and award-winning from all over the globe.

Freedom Restored

We had many travel companions on our pilgrimage. Friends, old and new, dear and distinguished collaborators whose presence made our journey all the more special.

When the project took shape, we were just coming out of the first lockdown period of the infamous 2020 pandemic, a complex, unprecedented time that painfully reminded us how the world is indeed one big family, where everything is connected.

I suffered greatly during this forced career break, though I was lucky to experience it with my family in a very privileged situation. But the worry was immense, as was the frustration with what was happening. Looking beyond the grave health and social wounds inflicted on the world, that global storm also wreaked great damage on art and culture, instilling toxic terror. Indeed, it also curtailed an essential value for human beings: freedom.

Solitude in and of itself is not negative at all. Just think of all the young women who decide to dedicate their lives to prayer, closed off from the world. However, in the case of the Covid-19 emergency in 2020, solitude and isolation were not a voluntary choice but rather an imposition. The state of solitude that could otherwise have brought about great spiritual benefits elicited the exact opposite effect.

Once freedom was restored, I was desperately raring to go out on my horse, gallop through open spaces, and breathe in nature. So, Veronica and I came up with the idea of going on a pilgrimage. I felt this strong need to regain the physical experience of a spiritual journey steeped in physical effort but also filled with the joyful variable of human contact.

Praying on the Road

For our ego, prayer is objectively a contradiction, a performance. And yet, the way I see it, the act itself brings with it great teachings, most of all, intellectual humility. This common, traditional practice of reciting the prayers we learned as children is much more important than it seems.

Why do we have to chant these fixed phrases from ancient memory? This is a question asked by children when forced to repeat their multiplication tables. Or piano students practicing their scales and arpeggios. Someday, when they have learned to count or become a pianist, those questions will seem idiotic to them.

In the presence of prayer, we remain children until our last breath. This is when we relate to God. I think it is only right to present ourselves to him with the utmost simplicity, in a manner that we could even define as childish. It remains an extremely powerful device for growth, as well as offering unexpected surprises.

There is a broad choice of manners and behaviors to adopt when addressing the Creator; for instance, praying from the heart in a silent, intimate, or explicit manner, addressing God as a father, at times, even complaining to him.

There is also praying "on the road," a devotional burst that involves physical effort, as taught by Saint Benedict. This is when we turn our attention to heaven while we are carrying out a task, especially a material task. I believe that God accepts any type of prayer as long as it is honest and sincere, as long as it has a good and just intention.

If you think about it, we are all travelers passing through this world. For each of us, life is a pilgrimage with a beginning and an end. Our existence is only a segment, a very brief segment, even if it lasts a hundred years. It is nothing compared to eternity.

When I think about the concept of traveling, the words of God come to mind: "Thou shalt love thy neighbour as thyself" (Mark 12:31 KJV), These words invite us to see our fellow man as a temple where God resides, so our destination is always the next person we come across.

There is a passage of a homily that captures this concept perfectly. I learned it from a great scholar, priest, and friend, Raniero Cantalamessa, who was a preacher to the papal household for three decades. I remember him saying: "Jesus was the first to suggest capital outflows abroad. However, he was not suggesting we transfer capital to some tax haven but rather to heaven. He even indicated who would be the porters to transport our assets where we can enjoy them for eternity: the poor. We are surrounded by them every day. So use them."

Faith and Rationality

There are strong similarities between the idea of pilgrimage and the journey of existence—the spiritual path of faith. I want to briefly mention this latter before metaphorically mounting my horse.

I consider myself a rational person. I studied law, and, by nature, I am not at all built for the transcendent experience. However, because I have a pragmatic approach intent on logical coherence, I have reasoned about what surrounds me. I see the universe as an immense mechanism like a clock. Everything proceeds according to perfect laws, just like the perfect rhythm of time marked by a clock. It goes without saying that life is governed by a supremely more elaborate, complex clock.

But there can be no clocks without clockmakers. No device can materialize out of nothing. Only a crazy person could believe that to be possible; all the more so if you look at the complex wonder of nature. It is logical, then, to perceive the presence of a holy demiurge, a transcendent architect who designed and created the universe (and us to populate it).

This was my first step toward faith in my late adolescence. I hope with all my heart that any skeptical readers out there can take this step too. It is impossible to believe that a human mind can embrace and grasp the essence of God, just as the robots we make will never be aware of who we, their creators, are, despite their immense abilities. On our earthly journey, we should be happy with gratefully observing creation with wonder and trusting in divine mercy.

If we were to believe Iago from Shakespeare's Othello, brought to the opera stage by 19th-century masterful Italian opera composer Giuseppe Verdi, when he says, "I believe in a cruel God who has created me like himself in anger of whom that I name," existence would be reduced to certain tragedy. I, on the other hand, am convinced that God is like any other father: a parent who loves his children with all his heart.

Solitude and Community

Though birthed quietly, the project quickly grew legs. When we told two director friends of ours, Paolo Sodi and Gaetano Morbioli, about it, they got excited. The plan expanded rapidly. From the idea of taking a few photos to capture some moments, it turned into getting over 150 people involved.

The fact that the journey embraced so many friends, musicians (mostly from other continents), collaborators, technicians, camera operators, and electricians did not weaken its deeper purpose. As a matter of fact, it enhanced it even further. Because things are never as good on their own. My sincerest thanks go to everyone who signed up for this wonderful, complex challenge. It became a shared journey with amazing intersections of stories, emotions, professional skills, and sparks of friendship.

Moments of notable, profound solitude (in the middle of the forests and natural parks, it is just you and your horse, nothing more) alternated with moments of community and sharing, just like wayfarers back in the day. After traveling for miles on foot, they would end their day around the hearth of an inn, honoring that moment of community and exchanging experiences, information, and purposes—a vital part of any pilgrimage.

For each leg of the journey, the schedule was two days on horseback along paths trodden over centuries, followed by a day's rest to let the horses recover and visit the spiritual places scattered along our route. And to pray in our manner: through music.

A blessing and a curse of the fame built up over almost thirty years in an artistic profession is that my personal affairs very seldom remain private. They tend to spread rapidly, involving other people and organizations, gaining a wider scope. In this case, the twenty-day journey became the subject of a film documentary produced by TBN (Trinity Broadcasting Network) through the producer Tom Newman. Our friends in the US had already filmed a Christmas special in Lajatico. They were so excited about this project that they wanted to film the journey. Their hope was to find positive and spiritual content to be shared globally, to bring optimism and faith back to communities tried and tested by this period of immense widespread suffering during the Covid 19 pandemic.

My staff and I had the privilege of relying on the advice of Father Enzo Fortunato, director of the press room of the Sacred Convent of Assisi, in finding inspiration for our route. In addition, the archbishop of Lucca, Monsignor Paolo Giulietti, gave us very valuable input. He also put us into contact with the heads of the dioceses we would pass through along the way. They were all gracious enough to agree to meet me and share their experiences with the pilgrims who came before me and hear their stories.

Finally, I also presented my project to Father Cantalamessa. It was he, with his customary generosity of soul, who suggested asking if the Holy Father would be available to bless us as we set out on our journey.

A long time ago, I wrote myself a personal prayer that includes the line: "Lord, make me an agent of your holy will." I often offer these words up to heaven, making myself available to God so that he can do with me as he sees fit. And many times, to my great pleasure and surprise, I realize how often it actually happens, as in the case of this pilgrimage. My horseback journey took on a broader scope, illuminated by our encounter with the Holy Father and many others, by the reflections that sprang up along the way, fostered by the hope of being more mature and spiritually richer than we were when we set out.

This journey has also given us the opportunity to stimulate a wide variety of people through the pages of this book to suggest meditating on the meaning of life, on its real purpose. That purpose, as Father Raniero Cantalamessa reminds us, is to do good, to send something up to the heavens, where one day we will deserve to find it.

Build or Destroy

We need strength, courage, and a strong will to pursue good, as it often goes against the inclinations of our bodies. The flesh moves downwards, pressed by the force of gravity, while the spirit rises.

It is hard to find balance in this dichotomy. But we have been given tools to help strengthen our spirit. The more tools we receive, the greater our responsibility to use them well. The Holy Scriptures tell us that "to whom much has been given, much will be required" (Luke 12:48 AMP.) It is up to each of us to choose how to use our talents, whether to use them for good or evil. On the other hand, good is to evil as the building is to destroy. Both require strength and ability. But building needs much more.

All you need to demolish a building is a pile of dynamite, whereas a lot more than that is needed to build one. The same goes for good and evil. The former requires strength, courage, and the spirit of sacrifice. After all, as a famous Chinese philosopher once put it, a falling tree makes more noise than a forest that grows. Those who do evil deeds make the news and immediately appear on the front page of all the print and digital newspapers and social media. Those who do good deeds act in silence, and almost no one ever finds out about them.

Just think about what is happening within the Church. A huge number of priests dedicate their lives to providing support in the poorest areas of the world, in contact with terrible sickness and misery. Who talks about them? Practically no one. On the other hand, there are priests who act very badly, and they are the ones who end up in the spotlight. We are all called upon to make our contribution to making the world a better place. Everyone can do it with the tools they have at hand and the talent that God gave them. I hope that this pilgrimage, this small spiritual act, can inspire many people.

A Privilege

I consider it a great gift and privilege to have a new traveling companion today. You, dear reader. Although you may not have lived experiences like mine, I hope that you can find the motivation within you to embark on your own pilgrimage with the path and means most suited to you. I think it can make us better people and help us recognize and joyfully experience the miracles happening around us every day.

Veronica and I decided to center this adventure on two themes. The first was paying homage to places of worship—sanctuaries and monasteries—catalysts of positive energy, where goodness has taken root through centuries of prayer. The second was music, a necessity of the spirit that can become a prayer, a tool of faith, thanks to its extraordinary capacity to speak directly to people's hearts.

In retrospect, I realize that on our own—as we had initially imagined the journey—we would have had an extremely difficult time and certainly would not have made it to the end. Once more, I have seen firsthand that dreams really do come true when there is a group desire when lots of people dream together.

We really wanted to embark on a pilgrimage that would make people stop and think about what matters. Thanks to the help of so many people, I can say "mission accomplished." It was a dream that became a reality, and it will stay with us forever, enshrined in the depths of our souls.

The days of our journey were full of open humanity. My wife and I learned so much: how to trust in others, how to trust in providence, and also how to transform fatigue into energy and positivity.

Traveling that stretch of the Via Francigena alongside Veronica and astride our four-legged friends, who were always able to sense our emotions and frame of mind, it was crystal clear to me that every journey can be a pilgrimage. Every true thought dedicated to life can remind us that we can be more than we are, restoring that "mind in love" Dante, Italian poet and writer, wrote about that highlights the divine seed (love) put back into each person's heart.

I pray that I can continue to perceive, at every sunrise and with the same energy, all that each foot of this journey whispered urgently in my ear: that life is the highest and most incredible manifestation of intelligent willpower and that it can lead to the path of God.

So, I would like to offer a brief note to the readers setting out on this journey. If you have the time and patience, you can find a more complex and personal assessment of the meaning of the pilgrimage in the appendix to this book. It is a "meditation" that I have written and rewritten over the years in an attempt to set down my reflections on the meaning of this earthly journey.

CHAPTER 1

From Saint Peter's Square to Sutri

The Eternal City

And so the journey begins. The alarm goes off at four, and we are in front of Saint Peter's Basilica by six.

Johann Wolfgang von Goethe—a German literary figure and an illustrious traveler of the 18th and 19th centuries—wrote: "For in this place the entire history of the world centers, and I count as a second birthday, the day…on which I entered Rome." We wholeheartedly wish for constant renewal, personal growth, and continual inner transformation for ourselves and for everyone. With this sentiment in our hearts, Veronica and I face this big first day of our journey setting out from the Eternal City.

We are heralded by the enchanting chorus of bells near and far chiming throughout the city's streets. These are joined by birds high in the sky greeting the sun and seagulls charting their flight path with a more assertive call. We also have the surreal delight of our beloved horses' hooves sounding out their steps along Rome's traditional *sampietrini* cobblestones.

It is particularly mild for May, and the city is deserted. We carry a small gift that we want to present to the Holy Father, a symbolic award that the Andrea Bocelli Foundation bestows upon exceptional individuals. It is a bronze sculpture in the shape of a pomegranate, designed to honor life as its sweet essence is preserved in each ruby seed of the fruit.

Rome on horseback! That in itself is a privilege that will be worth all our efforts and exertions. With this thought in mind, I use the reins to practice the commands to get our Andalusian battle horses to bow before Pope Francis.

A light morning breeze welcomes us before the facade of Saint Peter's Basilica against the dazzling backdrop of Bernini's colonnade in this square that is the heart of Christianity and the destination of pilgrimages from all over the world.

Peace and Music

We proceed on horseback, as though it were centuries ago, to meet a great man of peace and also to pay homage to Saint Peter's tomb, to pray before the first of the apostles, the first of the popes, in the Vatican grottoes beneath the basilica's altar.

Peace is the first traveling companion that I want to mention: shared harmony, total lack of tension or conflict. Our wish, our fundamental prayer, is a global rejection of all wars. Because peace is, in and of itself, the most opportune and obvious thing man should seek. Whereas conflict—still afflicting so many countries around the world—is nothing but an intellectual mishap. Nonetheless, man has never fully understood this. It is a mystery how human beings, the intelligent entities that they are, cannot find a way past this obstacle.

I am certain that most of the human race wants peace, an end to violence, and for us all to live decently, in a position to develop our individual potential. Turning these hopes into the tangible energy of individual action is what truly matters. This commitment requires courage (from the Latin *cor habeo*, "having heart"). Courage is the virtue of fortitude, defined as constancy in the pursuit of the good, as the ancient Greek philosopher Plato taught us. Each one of us is called upon to make our contribution to help life find its highest expression in peace and harmony.

Art communicates the incommunicable. Through an encoded message, it expresses what we are unable to say through written or verbal language. That is what music is. Music is arithmetical. All of its components—the notes—can be reduced to numbers: duration, intensity, and pitch. Every musical masterpiece can be expressed in numbers.

However, these numbers can never explain why people have emotional reactions to music. One great thinker/philosopher of the 17th and 18th centuries Gottfried Leibniz defined music as a "hidden exercise," as the human soul moves by an arcane principle. And long before, the German philosopher Aristotle noted music's potential to produce "a certain effect on" and change "the moral character of the soul."

In its substance and immediacy, music is an intangible experience of an invisible, but clearly perceptible, grace. It is a bridge providing instant and easy access to what lies behind the veil of everyday noise. Knowing the language of music is a useful skill, not only for those who work in the field. Music (like philosophy) arises from wonder in its infinitely different combinations of seven notes. It speaks to us through the divine gateways of our senses. From there, the soothing salve penetrates deep into our inner senses, where thoughts and intuitions are formed. It enters our soul, our truest essence. Music opens the doorway to the temple of our soul and reminds us that everything is sacred, that nature is supernatural, and that seemingly empty space is never actually empty.

In ancient Rome, the politician Marcus Porcius Cato urged legislators to ban soldiers from listening to music. He believed it had the power to soften their souls and render them unfit for combat. Now that we want to be rid of war, music could be a powerful tool for peace.

Any talent we have been gifted with can, and should, be put at the service of peace. This reminds me of the words of my elementary school teacher Ines Giamprini. A rare example of dedication to work and love for her students, she played a key role in my early education, both academic and spiritual. She said to me one day: "Remember, Andrea, that God gave you a gift, and this gift is not something you earned." It was a wise lesson that I have never forgotten.

Saint Peter's Square

Veronica and I leave our horses and approach the entrance to the basilica, hand in hand. We come up beside the central obelisk with its illusions of perspective, at an equal distance from the colonnade embracing Saint Peter's Square. Here we are greeted by the monk and journalist Enzo Fortunato (as we saw earlier, he's director of the pressroom of the Sacred Convent of Assisi). This brilliant man is blessed with the natural gift of enjoying his faith with contagious delight. He guides us to Saint Peter's tomb.

Emiliano and my daughter, Virginia, are also with us. Moved by our surroundings, we walk through this colossus. It is the largest church in the world, with a total surface area of twenty-three thousand square meters, forty-five altars, eleven chapels, ten thousand square meters of mosaics, and dozens of master-pieces, including Italian sculptor and archictect Gian Bernini's bronze baldachin and Italian sculptor and painter Michelan-gelo's extraordinary *Pietà*.

Showing my daughter this sculptural miracle means so much to me. Many years ago, I was given the extraordinary opportunity to visit and even touch the sculpture. The super-visor at that time allowed me to climb up onto a platform for a few moments and use my hands to see the magnificence of that Madonna and Christ. I was deeply unsettled by the face of the Virgin Mary. Michelangelo sculpted her as a mere eighteen-year-old to symbolize the essence of pure spirit impervious to the laws of aging. After listening to my thoughts on the immea-surable scope of the genius behind such creation, the supervi-sor said to me: "Every now and then, the Lord enjoys pouring a few drops of himself into one of us to remind the rest of us of our mediocrity." It is hard to argue with that. Just think of Dante's *Divine Comedy*, Bach's cantatas, or Mozart's sympho-nies. I am delighted that my daughter can now experience the same wonder I felt that day, wonder at such perfection blend-ing inspiration, idea, and technique.

Out in the open air once more, we take our horses and enjoy once again the excitement of trotting down Via della Conciliazione to the musical pitter-patter of hooves on cobblestones. The air is sweet-smelling and mild, feeling sacred to us on this special day. We go back to the square and meet Cardinal Mauro Gambetti. Right on schedule, thirty minutes later, the Holy Father leaves the Domus Sanctae Marthae and comes to meet us.

We imagine people who make history, key figures for all of humanity—like the Pope—to be constantly focused on resolving important and complex problems from sunrise to nightfall. Slightly abashed and extremely happy, I appreciate this gesture of infinite generosity from Pope Francis. He has found time out of his busy day to greet us, to gift us with rosary beads—as he often does to the people he meets—and to bless us as we set off on our pilgrimage, a journey that he clearly also thinks can prompt many people to reflect on the meaning of life, on faith, and on crucial issues that often get lost in everyday life.

The Pope welcomes us with a smile that radiates hope and confidence. The first to run to him is Virginia, who is so excited to meet him. She has been told many times about her immense privilege of receiving his blessing when she was just a baby. The Holy Father seems amused by this unorthodox but very affectionate greeting. He exchanges some words with each of us, shakes our hands, thanks us, and presents us with rosary beads, giving us his blessing. Pope Francis is an extremely charismatic man. His presence moves you. His honest goodness and authenticity are transmitted through his voice, demeanor, and simple gestures. These gestures are the result, aim, and strength of an immensely cultured person who also has great humanity.

Throughout my career—spanning over a quarter of a century now—I have had the pleasure of an audience with more than one pope. But this meeting with Pope Francis restored a sense of humanity in me that is almost unfathomable. I had a very emotional reaction the day he was elected. I was on vacation with two childhood friends and happened to find myself in front of a television when the vote was being announced. When the new pope spoke, uttering those memorable words that many of us know well, I couldn't help crying. I was a bit embarrassed because I was there with two people who had known me all my life and yet had never seen me cry. So that is my small "grievance" with the Holy Father!

Forty-Eight Red Roses

We are ready to leave the capital and set off on our journey. On horseback, we head across the Aelian Bridge at the foot of Castel Sant'Angelo (also famous for being the dramatic setting of the final act of Giacomo Puccini's opera *Tosca*). I am astride a black courser, Nevado, my favorite horse who has won many prizes over his lifetime. Crossing that bridge over the Tiber, for a moment, I forget proper etiquette and set off at a gallop. This means that Veronica has to rush after me to tell me off. And she is right to.

Then it is time to say goodbye to our little Virgi, who is returning to her studies in Forte dei Marmi. She will meet up with us again over the coming days in Sutri and other stops along the way. As will Matteo and Amos, as long as their work commitments allow it.

I always carry my three children with me, even when they are not physically present. They are my top priority and my greatest joy. They come before everything and everyone else. This is not hyperbole; it is a simple, powerful truth, as any father or mother knows well. They have had a huge influence on me, on how I view life and love, and even on my way of performing. The path you take when you become a parent is electrifying. It stimulates a major transformation within you. I have tried to be a diligent and loving father, though the time I get to spend with them is always less than I would like due to my career. However, it must be said that if you organize things well—as in this case—you can always find time to spend with your loved ones. Besides, the quality of time you spend with them is far more important than the quantity.

We are also joined by our friend Pasquale Beretta, who wanted to be by our side throughout the journey. One of my most beloved horses, Caudillo—an animal with great international performances in his past—came from Pasquale's stables. Today is also a special day for Pasquale. He keeps telling us that he will never forget it. Not so long ago, his business involved delivering up to a thousand horses a year to Argentina. Ever since Jorge Mario Bergoglio of Argentina became pope, Pasquale and his wife have longed for the chance to meet him and get a rosary blessed by him. Pasquale had expected a quick greeting that morning; he certainly did not think that the Holy Father would take the time to exchange some words with him in his native tongue.

As soon as he receives the beads from the hands of Pope Francis, he immediately thinks of his beloved wife. He won't be able to be with her on their forty-eighth wedding anniversary coming up in less than a week, so he gives the rosary beads to a friend who is on his way up to Lombardy, and thus gets them to his wife, along with forty-eight red roses, on the anniversary of their vows. An extremely poetic act that would bring her great joy.

Living poetically means living for goodness. You need to pursue harmony in order to achieve this. Not just musical harmony. You must be in tune with the world and spiritually interpret the mystery of our earthly journey. This is the only way to understand how wonderful and miraculous it is to be alive.

So here we are, starting out on our enterprise, a journey where it would be crucial to surrender ourselves to attain the serenity of those who know that a higher hand is guiding our passage. In every moment of our daily lives, we are "forced" to put our trust in something or someone, though perhaps unconsciously. When we walk down the street, we have to hope that the cars are being driven by sober, capable people fully focused on their driving. It only takes a second for a life to end. When we go to the hospital with a health issue, we must trust that the doctor can figure out the actual cause, make the right diagnosis, and give the correct treatment. So much is out of our hands.

The Accident

About ten miles outside Rome, we come to the ruins of the Etruscan city of Veii in the medieval town Isola Farnese. This ancient city was prosperous thanks to its control of the salt mines. Described by the Roman historian, Tito Livio as a *pulcherrima urbs* (beautiful city) and comparable to Athens in its size, Veii was conquered by the Romans in the fourth century BC. Despite its vicinity to urbanized areas, the Veii regional natural park has conserved a green belt around Rome. It has a wild and authentic quality to it. Hills, forests, waterfalls, and pastures wind around the vestiges of the Etruscan-Roman civilization, among the ruins of the necropolis and the drainage channels dug into the tuff rock.

We pass by the waterfalls and head toward the natural park. An hour later, we reach the earthly paradise where spring calls out to our hearts.

Everything seems to be going swimmingly when we suddenly hear a shout. Veronica stops and turns quickly. Then she, too, lets out a shout. "Oh, my God! Andrea! He is dying!" I don't understand who she is talking about, so I think it must be one of our traveling companions.

Veronica starts to cry. "Our little horse! Our little horse is dying!"

"What's going on?" I ask impatiently.

"Caudillo is dying!" she cries, climbing down off her horse and thrusting the reins at me as she rushes over to the scene of the accident. Barbara, our guide, who had been riding up ahead, realizes that something is wrong and turns back. My little horse Caudillo, who was being ridden by Pasquale that day, had stumbled upon a hidden manhole along the pebbled road. It collapsed under his weight, and the horse ended up with his entire leg stuck in the pipe underneath. It was going to be impossible to pull him out. When a horse gets stuck with its legs bent in on itself, it just cannot get up again. It needs room to push itself up. If it can't get up, it starts to panic and can really hurt itself with its desperate movements.

After just a few seconds, Caudillo looks like he has just swum across a river; he is terrified and dripping with sweat. Acting with extreme bravery, Emiliano wedges himself in under the horse's head, holding him as still as possible to stop Caudillo from fatally injuring himself.

A couple of hundred feet up ahead, I am shaken by the desperate cries of those trying to help poor Caudillo. Someone suggests calling roadside assistance to harness the horse and pull him out of his mortal trap. Meanwhile, I stand there holding the reins of Nevado and Veronica's horse, Girasol, a white, blue-eyed Spanish horse. I pray for my poor traveling companions, pray that they can find a solution, as unlikely as it seems. In the meantime, the rest of the group gradually arrives at the scene. Everyone is trying their best to help, but what can they do? Emiliano is crying, Pasquale is crying, Veronica is crying and running for help in spite of her sore knee.

Our film crew stayed behind that day. However, they are following us with a drone, and they can see from the footage that something has gone wrong. But they can't get to us by car on that road. So, one of the director's team grabs a huge case of first aid equipment for extreme situations, including an ax and some harnesses. He runs up the road and finally reaches us.

Thirty minutes go by, and it seems like an eternity. Then, suddenly, God knows how, but thanks to everyone's help, our beloved Caudillo is freed and manages to pull himself out. His leg doesn't seem to be broken. Unable to put any weight on it, the horse hobbles to the truck with Emiliano's help and climbs up into it with great effort. He is brought immediately to a vet, where he is examined and treated. An hour later, we get word: his tendons were damaged, and the leg had to be put in plaster. Basically, the horse is alive and will get better. Maybe he would no longer be the Caudillo that everyone admired for his skill and training, but he would still receive all our love and affection. In fact, just a few months later, Caudillo was walking again, recovered to full health.

Along Via Cassia

After the incident with Caudillo, we arrive at Campagnano and the Santuario Madonna del Sorbo, immersed in greenery. According to local legend, the church was founded following a miracle and an apparition of the Virgin Mary. We go in and say a prayer of thanks before the altar featuring an icon of the Virgin and Child. We join in the rosary, and at the end, I sing Schubert's "Ave Maria," accompanied by the organ.

This score is an example of how music is a mysterious gift that often transcends the intentions of the person behind it. Some songs are initially conceived with a message that is then surpassed by the intrinsic expressive character of the composition, like Christianity's most famous musical prayer. Franz Schubert wrote the music in 1825 as the sixth in a series of seven *Lieder* taken from the verses of the epic poem *The Lady of the Lake* written by Walter Scott, one of the fathers of Romanticism. The original text was not the canonical prayer to Mary, but as the composer himself wrote in a letter, this hymn "grips every soul and turns it to devotion." I believe that the Virgin Mary helped us that day in a situation that could have easily turned into a tragedy, for my horse and for the work of so many people. Over one hundred people, between crew and friends, were already giving their all in those first stages of the journey.

Along the ancient Via Cassia, built by a Roman consul around twenty-three centuries ago (in medieval times, its first seventy-four miles were part of the Via Francigena pilgrim route), we pass by Monterosi, once an important center of trading and cultural exchange between Romans and Etruscans.

We are tired and exhausted from the incident with the horse, but morale remains high among the group. Spring's song is in the air, and nature calms us and whispers to us soothingly. Trees, flowers, and meadows quietly grow around us. The sun's rays follow us. The intensity of their heat is regulated by whatever foliage they encounter on their journey downward.

Immersed in this luxuriant natural beauty, we recover the right spiritual perspective to regain inner peace and reflect on where we are and why we have set out on this journey.

Peace is the missing ingredient for making the world an earthly paradise for everyone. Every argument and every violation of peace is a setback caused by a short circuit. It shows that our neurons have malfunctioned in some manner. This simple observation is based on something I believe we have all experienced.

How many times have you stopped yourself just on the verge of anger, biting your tongue to keep yourself from blurting out something, then an hour later, realizing that it wasn't actually something that needed to be said? A day later, you may not even remember what it was that had annoyed you in the first place or the reason for your simmering desire to hurt someone. Then, if you think about the episode further down the road, you realize that you dodged a bullet, and those words that you managed to bite back would have been foolish and pointless.

All disputes can be avoided. If we want them to be avoided between nations and peoples, then we must begin in our own individual lives. We are all guilty; let's be honest. We all act foolishly at times. We all say things we regret. When this happens, we must plainly and honestly see it as an intellectual mishap, as I said before.

In the meantime, along the Via Francigena, we have the privilege and gift of sharing stories and meeting men and women who know and live in peace and who aspire to peace. Stories are often shared in a situation like our pilgrimage, which remains private at all times, whether we are nearly alone or whether there are dozens of us.

One such story came from our interpreter, with whom Veronica and I chatted over a cup of coffee. He is an American with a very moving story. A police officer when he was young, he moved to Italy to follow God's will.

There is also our guide Barbara, who delegated the task of leading us on the road (with all its points of peril, including forests and paths along sheer cliffs with cars whizzing past us). Barbara lives in harmony with the horses. She was already very familiar with a stretch of the Via Francigena and had also traveled along the route before our journey to study it and best assess the various options. To follow us, or rather to lead us, she had decided to temporarily suspend the steady job that she had held at a farm for years. When we arrive in Valdera, she will tell us: "It's all clear to me now. Now that I am on the road, I have decided to keep going." And sure enough, when we reach our destination at the end of our journey, Barbara will continue on to France.

The pilgrimage is a crucial journey for her as well. She really felt its effect. Indeed, Barbara has now changed her profession and continues to ride horses, not at a farm but along the ancient paths of the Via Francigena.

Sutri

Excavated into the tuff rock of a hill looking out over the Roman road Via Cassia and named after the ancient patrician family (*gens Cassia*), Sutri casts a spell on us with all the history in the air and the beauty of the town. We can feel the vortex of time in the Etruscan necropolis bumping up against medieval walls, in the alleyways, and the magnificent beauty of the Santa Maria Assunta co-cathedral (constructed in the twelfth century around older sacred buildings).

We have a very special traveling companion for the final stretch of our journey, Michael W. Smith, riding an American quarter horse (a cross between a Mustang and an English thoroughbred) owned by Beretta. Known in the US as "Smitty," Michael is a peer of mine, a musician of great talent and success. Singer, composer, piano and guitar player, he is one of the world's most famous Christian music artists. And he is an excellent equestrian, as I tell him with my sincerest admiration. He is also a great nature lover. Indeed, he lives on a farm just outside Nashville.

Michael, Veronica, and I muse on the peace around us and the constant miracles that nature presents to us without our awareness most of the time. We are so busy with all our little concerns, missing out on the truest and most profound meaning of life. Michael hints at his troubled past, how he lost his way as a young man before turning a new leaf and realizing his responsibility as an artist and as a man called to do good in the world. He shares this beautiful, cheerful message with us, opening our hearts.

Sutri is a marvel that never ceases to amaze. It boasts the caves of Orlando, the French champion that legend has it was born here, and the house where Dante stayed on his way to Rome for the jubilee in 1300. I have the immense pleasure of meeting here with my long-time friend, the art critic and well-known politician Vittorio Sgarbi. Among his many jobs, he is also the mayor of Sutri and has decided to award me honorary town citizenship that day. The air of friendship and trust on this occasion is very special with Vittorio and his partner, Sabrina, along with his sister, the filmmaker and editor El Sabetta Sgarbi.

It was thanks to Vittorio that I met the love of my life. The date was May 8, 2002, though it was raining like a day in winter. At the insistence of my agent, I went to Vittorio's fiftieth birthday party that day despite the weather. At that time, he was a member of parliament. By pure coincidence, Veronica was also there. A friend had invited her along. Only a few minutes after briefly chatting with her, I dedicated a love song— "Occhi di fata"—to her. I think she may have been flattered. But apart from the song, we fell in love instantly.

When we first met, she was only vaguely aware of who I was and had no interest in the personal lives of public figures. She knew nothing about my life (and wasn't remotely interested in it). However, by the end of that evening, a single handshake had transformed our lives. As I like to say, chemistry spoke for us, a force to be reckoned with that cannot be escaped. Life decides for us, and we just need to be brave enough to listen. A suggestion, a touch, we sensed a strong vibration, and destiny showed us the way.

We meet up again with Vittorio in Sutri today, exactly nineteen years later. In the intervening years, Veronica and I have made our wedding vows, bound by our long journey together. We have struggled, faced headwinds with open arms, lived together, and spent twenty-four hours a day with each other. Even now, at the dawn of every day, we renew our wish to be by each other's side. My companion, friend, lover, partner in happiness and pain, my wife is the electricity that injects energy into everything in my life and makes everything work.

A relationship requires commitment, enthusiasm, a good dose of patience, and plenty of affection. As with many similar species, in their natural state, humans would tend toward polygamy (a reflection of mine that has been intentionally misinterpreted by some journalists in the past). Men and women with a more evolved and aware spirit have, however, understood the moral wholesomeness of monogamy. Two people who love one another know the pain that betrayal would cause to their partner, both aware of the damage it would inflict. I believe that it is right to formalize this promise of loyalty and devotion before God. And I believe that fulfilling that promise is an art.

To give our horses some time to rest, we spend another day in Sutri and make some time for music. The director recording our pilgrimage, Paolo Sodi, steps aside for Gaetano Morbioli, who specializes in filming musical events. During this pause in our journey, Virginia comes to meet us from Forte dei Marmi.

We also meet up with friends and collaborators, including the producer Tom Newman along with Marco Marchesi and Luca Casini.

The young, immensely talented French soprano Clara Barbier is also there. She was the first student to receive the Community Jameel and Andrea Bocelli Foundation scholarship for London's Royal College of Music. That support allowed her to join the famous RCM Opera at one of the world's finest conservatories. Seeing her growing success brings us great satisfaction. Clara is a tangible example of the concept of empowerment, which is a top priority in the projects of the Andrea Bocelli Foundation (ABF).

Together with Clara and Michael, we head over to Sutri's Roman amphitheater at dusk. This immense structure dates back two thousand years, an archaeological monument of stunning beauty with its oval form and three tiers of steps. Thousands of lanterns light up the site while I have the pleasure of performing some music for the cameras of the US Christian TV station TBN, which is kindly and respectfully accompanying us on our pilgrimage. Dressed up in concert attire and even happier after the win of my soccer team, Inter Milan, just witnessed on television, I stand on the stage of the amphitheater. In this exalted setting, suspended out of time by this masterwork, I start by singing Francesco Paolo Tosti's "Preghiera," with Michael Smith accompanying me on the piano.

This composer's body of work of vocal music (over four hundred songs written in Italian, English, French, Neapolitan, and Abruzzese) makes him the only Italian artist on the same level of composers such as Schubert, Schumann, and Fauré. An intellectual man and friend of Verdi, Puccini, and Mascagni, he was also a singing teacher at the Royal English Court (where his students included Nellie Melba and Enrico Caruso). This tormented "Preghiera" is a musical supplication that finds perfect harmony with the verses of the Tuscan Risorgimento poet Giuseppe Giusti, the writer of famous works satirizing politics and society.

The concert continued with Clara joining me. We sing "Pianissimo" by Mauro Malavasi (both this and the previous song are from my album *Believe*), a love letter that embraces both earthly and divine emotions. It is an imagined dialogue between a couple who see the hand and love of God in the tenderness of their love. As often is the case in the productions of our friend Malavasi, the piano plays a prominent role in backing up the intertwined melodies of the duet.

The evening ends with a cake and candles that Vittorio Sgarbi is called to blow out. We celebrate his birthday, which, as I said before, is also the anniversary of the day I met the love of my life.

CHAPTER 2

From Sutri to Lake Bolsena

Toward Viterbo

Today's itinerary is twenty-two miles along roads and paths in the northern part of Lazio, where the landscape gets softer and starts to take on a more Tuscan feel. By nightfall, we will reach Viterbo, the "city of the popes." This wonderful capital of La Tuscia holds its long story in its name (*Vetus Urbs*, old city). An alternate papal residence, Viterbo hosted a dozen popes in the second half of the thirteenth century. Lavish traces of this regal past greet visitors arriving in Piazza San Lorenzo, overlooked by the Papal Palace. Its Gothic loggia was where the Holy Father would face his people, and its famous conclave room held the longest papal election in history: over one thousand days of deliberation and counting votes.

This stretch of the Via Francigena that we are currently traveling along is one of the most spectacular of the entire pilgrimage. Forests taken straight from Northern European fairy tales boast vast numbers of conifers that bear no resemblance to a Mediterranean landscape. We ride along white roads free of branches and scattered with handy springs where we stop every now and then to let our horses drink.

After Capranica and Lake Vico, which, at an altitude of 1,600 feet, keep vigil over the Cimini mountain range, a real surprise awaits us at San Martino al Cimino. This medieval village's Cistercian abbey has an organ that I am given permission to play.

It is an organ just like the one in the small San Leonardo church in Lajatico, where I first experienced the amazement and strong emotional impact of the acoustics of this instrument. I was only around four or five, yet I understood straightaway that those sounds were a call to reflection, a mysterious instrument whose voice guided my attention to heaven, stimulating those crucial questions, those existential examinations that even children ponder. My first approach to the holy repertoire was on the keys of an organ. Its acoustics today still remind me of a natural devotion expressed by the community of the faithful.

Lajatico is a rural town, and its people expressed an authentic, gentle piety, singing hymns that I still carry in my heart.

The last stretch on horseback snakes through a forest. The path is steep, and our passage is made difficult by low-hanging thorny branches, steps, and low stone walls. The horses are forced to ride in a single file. As we exit the forest, Viterbo appears before us in its splendor. The cobblestones of its magnificent town squares mean we have to dismount and walk alongside our animal friends, strolling along among historical buildings and gurgling fountains. This city enchants visitors with its artistic and natural beauties, but it also snares people with its culinary delights, as we are about to find out.

The Prince and Forgiveness

Veronica and I have the honor (and joy) of riding through a forest of centuries-old beech trees with Prince Ermias Sahle Selassie, grandson of Emperor Haile Selassie of Ethiopia. He descends from the Solomonic dynasty, which some say is the oldest royal family in the world. Tradition claims it was founded by Menelik I, son of the Queen of Sheba and King Solomon of Israel (who was, in turn, the son of King David).

It is a precious opportunity to retrace the life, strong morals, and faith of his immense grandfather, the *negus neglect*, the king of kings, an important historical figure in the political events of the twentieth century. He was a man who cultivated the highest values, forgiveness above all.

"My grandfather had an exceptionally significant life, in both the good and the bad. He suffered exile and lived through war, but he never gave up thanks to the strength of his unshakeable faith," the prince tells us as we ride along.

Six years after becoming emperor of Ethiopia in 1930, Haile Selassie was ousted during the conflict with Italy under its fascist regime. He lived in exile until 1941 when he was able to return and regain his rule of the country. He was an enlightened monarch and a wise man who always had words of peace aimed at sowing concord and reconciliation, even with his own adversaries.

The words of the *negus*—just before he was deposed and then killed—in an interview with Italian journalist Oriana Fallaci really struck a chord with me: "History does not forget; men, on the other hand, can forget. They can also forgive if they have a good soul. And we try to be good. Yes, we have forgiven. But have never forgotten."

I, too, believe that forgiving does not mean forgetting. Forgetting numbs. Without memory, we cannot learn from life's journey. However, forgiveness remains a cornerstone of human piety and also of Christian religion.

Forgiving frees the soul. Forgiveness is an echo and consequence of love: one of its main effects. Without forgiveness, life can easily get stuck, shrivel up, and lose its glow. As Pope Francis observed, "Forgiveness is the essence of the love which can understand mistakes and mend them. How miserable we would be if God did not forgive us!"

An Act of Volition

The Gospel tells us to love our enemies, to overcome instances of hatred and treat our enemies as we would treat a friend, and to turn our resentment into love. (.)Matthew 5:44; Romans 12:21; Proverbs 25:21; Ephesians 4:31–32.) Not easy at all for us mortals, but not impossible if driven by an act of volition.

If peace is the main ingredient to make the world an earthly paradise, for every intellectual mishap that causes a rupture in the peace, we need a surgical intervention to restore it to the previous state, the status quo. This ingredient, this procedure that is often painful and complex—not least of all because of the energy required—is called *forgiveness*.

The worst sin a person can commit is not believing in heavenly mercy, thinking that God will not forgive us. This is the same mistake Judas made after sending his master to his death.

What really condemned him was his inability to believe in the possibility of forgiveness. (Matthew 27:3–5.)

During this pilgrimage, I reflected quite a bit on what Christian love really is and really comprises. Our Creator says you should love your neighbor as yourself, love your enemy as your friend. (Mark 12:31.) But we know that this is not humanly possible. It is highly unlikely that we can have the same feelings for someone who has caused us great harm that we have for a friend.

The answer I have reached is simple: On an emotional level, you cannot turn hate, rage, or dislike into love. In reality, you can love in the Christian sense, meaning treat an enemy as you would a friend. Embrace them rather than strike them. This is possible, though difficult. Perhaps you will continue to feel that aggressive impulse in your gut, but your brain can still tell your legs to go toward your enemy and embrace them. This is not hypocrisy but rather a deliberate effort, an act of volition. Love for your partner and loved ones is a different thing altogether.

But there is a compassion that our Christian conscience dictates and that we owe to our neighbors and our enemies, without exception.

Surprises Big and Small

We head north from Viterbo toward Bolsena and its majestic lake, which oversees pilgrims on their journey from Lazio to Umbria and Tuscany. We have to cross an underpass to get out of the town. Behind us lies the freeway, currently the scene of a minor pileup. We are relieved to be back on the gravel road, beautiful and silent, which soon presents us with a very different kind of mood. After just a few miles, I take advantage of this return to stillness to convince Veronica to ride my sharp and trustworthy horse Nevado. She leaves her own horse, who is forced to continuously trot to keep up with the other steeds, in the much more expert hands of Emiliano. I mount a young four-year-old stallion, Badillon. This reshuffle will be crucial if we want to get to the end of our pilgrimage without incident.

I stress the fact that horses are not tools but traveling companions. If you fail to fully grasp this concept, the horse itself will let you know. They each have their own temperament and sensibility, which quickly merge onto the same wavelength as the rider. At the end of our journey, I would jokingly scold Veronica for "shattering" my Nevado. That wasn't true, but the fact is that Nevado feels he has a greater responsibility with Veronica on his back.

He understands that he has to proceed more carefully and almost offers himself as a "sofa" for the rest of the journey. A horse's personality is the combination of its nature, training, and the influence of whoever is on its back. There are those who chomp at the bit and want to be at the front of the group, only slowing down when they are in the lead. Then there are those who proceed with the composure of a poised lady but, if urged, will set out at a gallop and pass the rest of the group.

Along the way, we stop at a waterhole so that the animals can quench their thirst. We meet some other pilgrims, exchanging some words and smiles. Our entire journey is dotted with encounters with other people, brief but intense moments full of humanity. There are many wonderful little surprises for my wife and me: the elderly racing pigeon enthusiast who wishes to show us the birds he trains; the quiet, aromatic pageant of the fields of poppies reaching toward the sky; the forests teeming with fireflies.

We stop at Montefiascone with its famous wines and the impressive medieval fortress Rocca dei Papi, conquered by Frederick Barbarossa, a Holy Roman Emperor in the 12th century, before returning under papal control in the early thirteenth century. From this spectacular panoramic viewpoint over La Tuscia—I can sense the scope, the incredible span, by just breathing in the pure air—we start off on the last few miles.

It is a fine and fairly easy path, apart from issues getting across a streamlet that our horses refuse to cross for no apparent reason. The first horse comes to a standstill, and then all the rest follow suit. We lose over half an hour here, and in the end, poor Emiliano, generous as always, has to dismount and wade through the stream, leading the horses across.

On the last mile, a blackthorn catches my neck, scraping my skin and leaving a visible mark. But thanks to the adrenaline, I don't even feel the sting.

Horse Riding at the Lake

Here we are at Bolsena, the "town of the eucharistic miracle," with Rocca Monaldeschi at its summit dominating the surrounding landscape. Its flights of steps and narrow streets lead through ancient stone buildings and town squares that unexpectedly appear in the maze of the medieval quarter. Lake Bolsena lies in front of the town. A peaceful body of water that formed 300,000 years ago, it is a watery ring rimmed by low, sandy shores and surrounded by fields, vineyards, vegetable gardens, and olive groves.

The people of Bolsena give us a warm welcome. The TV cameras record our arrival at the square in front of Santa Cristina Basilica. I decide to give my trusty four-legged companion (and myself) a special treat. I mount Nevado and ride him through the water. I then do the same with the horse who sired Nevado. Riding a horse through the shallow water is exhilarating. The lake is calm and quiet—perfect for this horse who likes water but is unsettled by waves, which there is no trace of here. He gallops happily, playing and kicking up sand, the lake at his ankles.

After a much-desired shower and dinner, Veronica puts aside her weariness and accepts my suggestion to go for a walk along the lake shore. The inadequacy of words is patent in this case. I can but scratch the surface of such moments, deep as the harmony and serenity enveloping us. Upon our return to the hotel, a light rain freshens the air and revitalizes the aromas of the vegetation.

After hearing of our arrival, some young musicians specializing in medieval music come up to Veronica and ask if I would come out onto the balcony to listen to them. I don't think it is fair to leave them out there in the rain, however, so I invite them inside to play in the hall, where I come down to meet them. Perhaps not the best idea, as their drums and bagpipes in an indoor setting reach decibel levels that are difficult to take, for me and even more so for Veronica. Though open and smiling to everyone, she is fighting a relentless headache at this time. But the musicians from the medieval group are friendly and deserve an audience. At the end of this impromptu concert, we give them our sincerest thanks.

Nighttime Reading

A quarter of a century touring the world, frequently hopping from one time zone to the next, has escalated what was already a physiological predisposition of mine. I find it hard to fall asleep. My days end late into the night and start, where possible, in the late morning. This is one of the reasons my companion and I choose to sleep in separate rooms, so I don't disturb her rest.

But the pace of the pilgrimage means we have to stick to a strict schedule. I adhere to the timetable, but I cannot get myself to fall asleep any earlier. So, reading is my trusty friend tonight, as on all other nights. Afterward, I listened to the radio and wrote my habitual email to Veronica (to share my reflections with her or to send her some verses I dedicated to her). I have also been keeping a journal for the past few years, where I scrupulously note the events of the day. It is no wonder that the night is held in great esteem by those who pen popular wisdom known as proverbs. It is a precious time, less polluted by distractions and noise, when we can study, think, or pray.

I am an avid reader, and I prefer to read at nighttime (as I just mentioned). I am not a big fan of audiobooks recorded by professional actors. I prefer the impersonal voice of speech synthesis. It renders the digital book without inflections or emotional conditioning. I always set the reading speed fairly fast. In fact, any of my friends who have heard it deem it unintelligible. But I am used to it.

Books can turn out to be extraordinary friends, enriching us spiritually and even changing our lives if read at the right time.

One of my favorite books is undoubtedly the Gospel, a limit-less treasure trove and the highest moral philosophy of them all. Then comes the Divine Comedy. I have been cultivating this passion for Dante's masterpiece ever since I was a little boy. I have even learned some of the cantos by heart.

Key writers in my formation as a reader and as a man were the great Greek philosophers and the seventeenth-century genius Blaise Pascal with his illuminating *Pensées*. Then come the masters of literature, like Alessandro Manzoni (with his unforgettable passionate pages on the conversion of the Un-named); Leo Tolstoy (fundamental for me are his *Resurrection* and *Confession* and his correspondence with Mahatma Gandhi); *Les Misérables* by Victor Hugo, an extraordinary treatise on the eternal struggle between good and evil; and Antonio Fogaz-zaro. Studying the life and thoughts of Buddha has also helped me better understand the similarities with Christianity. There are also contemporary scholars whom I have had the honor of meeting in person and whose philosophy I have discovered through their books: Arturo Paoli, Chiara Amirante, and Ra-niero Cantalamessa.

I also recently read the work of the Italian mystic Maria Val-torta, who lived from 1897 to 1961. After reading about the dire circumstances of her life trapped in a painful, paralyzed body contrasted with her spiritually advanced condition enlightened by divine decree, I have no doubts. The voice of Maria Valtor-ta, resounding from the pages written on her sickbed, is the expression of a divine voice. For those familiar with the Holy Scriptures and who believe in the Gospel's message, Valtorta's writings deliver the dizziness of a powerful experience, even disturbing at times. But even those without the gift of faith and those who struggle to grasp the enigmas of transcendence cannot help but be impacted by such a masterpiece.

The Holy Child

Visiting Santa Cristina Basilica in Bolsena is one of the most moving moments of the entire pilgrimage. I am particularly delighted to have Virginia alongside me. She is back with us again from Forte dei Marmi. The basilica's charm is amplified by the hints of the events that took place within these sacred walls, evoking strong emotions in visitors.

With thousands of years of life and history, the church contains the mortal remains of Saint Christina of Bolsena, the child saint. Veronica and I, alongside our daughter, pray together before her tomb, reflecting on the inner strength of someone who sacrificed her life in the name of an ideal and religious faith.

We enter the sanctuary under its tripartite facade. The Romanesque interior has three apses with a cross-shaped vault. The right-hand nave is dominated by a sixteenth-century wooden crucifix. The left-hand side features a chapel dedicated to Saint Christina, with her relics stored in an urn on the altar. A cave carved into the rock leads to the catacombs, where the sarcophagus with the martyr's remains was discovered in the late nineteenth century.

Let's go back to the time of Emperor Diocletian. The daughter of Urbano, the *magister militum* of Bolsena, Christina is still a child when her father locks her up in a tower along with other girls to act as vestal virgins for a pagan cult. But Christina has already discovered and joined Christianity. She refuses to venerate the idols there and instead destroys them. She is arrested and tortured but comes out unharmed, thanks to divine intervention.

She is then condemned to death by drowning in Lake Bolsena. However, she miraculously survives because the large rock around her neck begins to float her toward the shore rather than drag her under. After more torments and more miracles, Christina succumbs, destroyed by the torture ordered by her own father and then by his successors. But she never recants. She is unshakeable in her faith.

According to Christian tradition, another important miracle occurred in the same basilica. The so-called Eucharistic miracle of Bolsena took place here in 1263, which led to the local Feast of Corpus Christi being founded a year later. A priest called Pietro da Praga is tormented by doubts about the doctrine of transubstantiation of the Eucharist (the turning of bread and wine into the body and blood of Christ), so he sets out on a long and difficult pilgrimage to strengthen his faith.

On the road to Rome, he stops off at the Bolsena sanctuary and says mass. At the moment of the consecration, he prays fervently for the gift of faith in the mystery of the consecrated host and the communion. Then when he breaks the host, he sees some scarlet drops falling from it. Blood drips onto the priest's corporal. We still have traces of this blood that was analyzed back then by a commission of theologians led by Thomas Aquinas and sent by the Pope.

The Inexplicable

There are so many things that our minds cannot understand or rationally explain; however, we can "experience" them by eagerly letting go. We are dulled by all the information that inundates our senses, information that we rely on and treat as important. And yet evidence would suggest that these senses are deceptive and misleading. Think of all the music arriving from overseas, saturating the air, broadcast by thousands of antennae. Yet our ears hear none of it. If we didn't have the tools to decipher those sounds, no one would believe in their existence. If you were to go back in time to the seventeenth or eighteenth century and tell people about these things (which nowadays we take for granted), you would probably end up burnt at the stake as a madman.

We are quick to trust our senses, and yet we have absolutely no trust in what our consciences suggest to us on a daily basis. Of course, it is hard to confront your conscience because it is uncomfortable; your conscience is too sincere. Far too often, anything we cannot understand—the extraordinary design of the universe and everything that was created for us—is dismissed as "chance."

I cite the words of Max Planck, winner of the Nobel Prize in physics in 1918, musician, philosopher, and originator of quantum physics: "All matter originates and exists only by virtue of a force which brings the particle of an atom to vibration and holds this most minute solar system of the atom together. We must assume behind this force the existence of a conscious and intelligent mind. This mind is the matrix of all matter."

Throughout the twentieth century, quantum theory opened up scenarios that were fascinating, to say the least, by fully exploring the infinitely tiny. I am not a scientist, and yet even I can perceive the dizzying heights of the topics and experiments implied by Planck's words. Consider the concept of the quantum field, for example, an energy field that occupies space (once believed empty), passing through it with its fluctuations. Or the phenomenon of quantum entanglement that occurs when two particles are intrinsically linked, a union that affects the physical system, with any actions or measures on the former also impacting the latter, and vice versa.

Above all, there is the suggestion of a huge step toward verifying that when the physical body ends its journey, the immortal conscience moves forward. I am reminded of Saint Augustine's words: "Miracles are not contrary to nature, but only contrary to what we know about nature."

Chance is a tempting concept that leads us to believe that anything we cannot understand is not true. In truth, we understand very little. Our mind, compared to the rest of our conscience, is like a bucket of water next to the sea. The great theologian, missionary, and friend of mine, Arturo Paoli, once told me something that I took to heart. He said that if we look closely at human tragedies, they all originate from what the ancient Greeks called *hýbris*, which means pride, conceit, and arrogance. The great works of classical tragedy teach us that the spark that ignites human catastrophes nests in pride, a feeling that is the enemy of reason, as well as faith. Faith is capable of annihilating pride. It is the overture to a life full of grace and beauty.

The entire universe is in constant communication. Nothing is lost. Every action begets a reaction, which means that if we propagate evil, it will spread like a wave, all unseen by us. Tomorrow or a year, or a decade from now, it will come back to the source, raining down repercussions. But the good news is that the same goes for goodness.

The Trappist Nuns

Along the stretch of road between Lazio and Tuscany, we can't resist stopping at the Vitorchiano Trappist Monastery, a special place of prayer inhabited by women of the faith. There are about seventy nuns here of all ages with the most diverse backgrounds. They all took their vows to fulfill their desire to discover the mystery of our Creator and experience his love.

We are blown away by their contagious joy. The rather sterile convent building is warmed by the smiles of the sisters. They emanate enthusiasm. In this celebratory atmosphere, I get ready to sing for them and with them. I warm up my vocals in the dressing room they provide for me and then walk through the church, with the nuns filling its wooden choir stalls at each side. I choose "Ave Maria." Accompanied by the organ and the flute, the nuns' voices sing along with mine in the counter melody composed by César Franck.

Veronica and I leave this visit fully refreshed. Together we reflect on the joy permeating this community, which, on the surface, could be wrongfully framed in suffering and darkness. Someone once said that smiling requires effort, commitment, and an act of volition. As happens when you look in a mirror, only if you smile will you receive a smile in return. My advice is that we should be the first ones to offer others a smile for no apparent reason. Life will smile back at us.

CHAPTER 3

From Bolsena to Sant'Antimo Abbey

Friends Forever

We receive a lovely unexpected visit from our friend Cristiano Quarratesi. He travels with us for a dozen or so miles as we head toward Radicofani. Cristiano was just eighteen when I taught him how to ride a horse, sparking a passion that has never left him and that even had an impact on his career. Uniting his love of medicine with his love of animals, he has become an excellent vet.

As we ride our horses along the green paths on this jubilant, fragrant day in May, we reflect on our lives and the small community that raised us. Our dominant feeling is undoubtedly that of gratitude. Lajatico is a small country village like many others around it in the Valdera area. It did not have many distractions to offer young men like us chomping at the bit. However, it made us into men. It drilled into us an array of values that gave depth to our lives, offering us a moral compass to guide us on our journey through life.

We recall old times, our carefree adventures as friends, and our shared moments of great laughter. There were also some moments spiced with a pinch of recklessness. One time I managed to convince my father to lend me his car, and I boldly taught Cristiano to drive. Then, with my young friend as a novice driver, we would set off for evenings of music in the bars of nearby towns. Our trailer got heavier by the month, laden with musical instruments and electronic devices.

I have very clear, tender memories of those years, making my long way up the ladder by working the region's piano bars. It taught me so much at both a professional and personal level. When I was a teenager, I initially only listened to classical music. In fact, my peers thought I was some kind of alien. They could recite by heart the songs of whatever singers were currently trending. When I first put myself forward to sing in a bar, they asked me, "How many songs do you know?" I replied: "I could learn three for this evening." And their answer was: "Come back when you have two hundred!" So, I ended up learning dozens of songs by different musicians and the most popular hits, ranging from Sinatra and Battisti to Elvis and The Beatles.

When I was around twenty, I started working as a pianist at piano bars to get a bit more financial independence and to pay for my singing lessons. I remember my first paychecks. I would earn around fifteen dollars an evening. I continued doing that until I finished my law degree. I used to work from Tuesday to Sunday, playing at bars and for private parties and ceremonies.

It was an interesting experience that was extremely useful on many levels. Having to tackle an immense catalog of international pop opened my eyes to a whole new world. I had to reevaluate my most stringent viewpoints. During those years, I realized that pop also has its masterpieces, its "classics."

At those bars, I would witness many moments of love blossoming, many couples spurred on by the emotion of the music. I, too, would often cross paths with some young girl with whom I would fall deeply in love, despite the precarious situation! But with all due respect to those early experiences with the female world, my network of solid male friendships held the greatest weight for me at that time, and they have lasted throughout the decades.

Friendship is another extraordinary form of love, and love generates understanding. Friendship is a sweet responsibility that requires commitment and self-sacrifice. It is, in fact, an essential part of my life. We confess things to our friends and reveal our most intimate secrets to them. Being friends is an act of recognition rarely based on words (usually, what does not need to be said is what matters most). It is understanding each other as we are, without pretense.

I have known many of my dearest friends since my early adolescence, and I still see them regularly, as often as my nomadic lifestyle allows, at least. There is a fresh burst of pleasure every time we meet. We take up where we left off—even if we have not seen each other for six months—as if we had never been interrupted.

For instance, there's my childhood friend Sergio Bartolini, my partner in thousands of tandem rides and races through the fields, so many summer holidays spent playing soccer or making slingshots. Or Adriano Fiaschi, my "second brother," along with Verano Belcari. In the sixties, we were an indestructible trio, between music, pranks, and staying out all night! We would spend endless evenings together, talking about everything and anything. We discussed love and pain but also higher matters, such as values or the dichotomy of being and appearing.

We would strum the guitar and dream about future artistic success. We'd spend evenings at my house joking around and writing songs (almost always love songs). After our customary late-night feeds of spaghetti, we would often go for a walk down to the river. As we tried to find our way through the dense country darkness, our roles would reverse, and I would be the one leading them.

We got into lots of mischief and played pranks together. Thinking about our antics today still makes me laugh with a pang of nostalgia. For instance, there was that time we all piled onto a Vespa and rode the long winding road downhill from Lajatico village to La Sterza. I was driving with Adriano behind me, acting as navigator, telling me when and where to turn. But we got caught. We passed the local bus, and the driver happened to be a friend of my father's. He reported us immediately, and I was in a lot of trouble that evening.

I have always been very close to my father. He was the one who taught me my determination to act rather than talk, my dedication to work, honesty, consistency, and my love of the land. However, we had very different personalities, and we would clash daily during those years.

I wore my hair long back then, like many of my friends at that time. But it was a sore point for my father. He just would not accept it and kept telling me to cut my hair. I would say, "But Dad, it suits me like this." And he would reply, "You only say that because you can't see yourself!"

Radicofani

We are in Tuscany at last. The Via Francigena crosses lengthwise through the province of Siena. Like a melodic line on a musical score, it unfurls along the hills of one of the world's most beloved and famous lands. We will journey through a large part of this segment of the mystical (and cultural and commercial) route dotted with little parish churches, abbeys, and castles. We will call at renowned towns such as San Gimignano, a miracle of medieval town planning with its fifteen towers, and Monteriggioni, a raised mirage that turns back time by eight hundred years. On our route map, we also have Sant'Antimo Abbey, an ancient monastery complex, and Bagno Vignoni, a thermal town that has been used since Roman times.

We set a fast pace on our journey today as we have a lot of ground to cover. We have a quick break for lunch in the small village of Ponte a Rigo in Val d'Orcia, where we are cordially welcomed by its mayor.

Our first stop is a place of overwhelming beauty and history, Radicofani. Here I can already get the scent of home. It is hard to put into words, but for me, Tuscany is like my "soul region." It is much more than just a geographical area. It is no wonder that Tuscany has been an idyllic reference for many centuries, a legendary place of discovery and later nostalgia for musicians, poets, painters, and dreamers from all over. Sure, you can visit it, but Tuscany must, above all, be experienced.

Its picture-postcard landscapes can only partially express the range of emotions that animate those privileged enough to breathe in its air. At the risk of indulging in parochialism, I believe that there is nowhere like it in the world thanks to its architectural, pictorial, sculptural, and panoramic wonders. It also has a wonderful capacity to provide refuge for the spirit. Its earth is blessed by flourishing nature, perfect for finding silence and reflection.

I must admit I was surprised by Radicofani's profound beauty and its spectacular castle, which has been restored to its old splendor for some years now thanks to some significant restructuring work.

After the long climb up to the foot of the medieval fortress, we rest at a small bar whose owners treat us to coffee. We are also greeted by the mayor, who offers to act as our guide. The fortress looms over the valley from a spur of basalt rock at almost three thousand feet.

We climb once more, this time by foot, and reach the summit of the castle. I fight my way to the highest parapet, up to the tower battlements. Here I have one of the most intense experiences of the journey. The day is warm and sunny, the air is clear, and the sounds of nature fill the surrounding area. Though Veronica is getting worried and tries to get me to come down, I remain here and feel like I am in heaven.

Faith and Family

In the meantime, our American friends from the Trinity Broadcasting Network continue to follow our pilgrimage with their usual restraint. They, too, fall in love with what this slice of Italy has to offer its visitors. Matthew and Laurie Crouch, famous figures (and producers) of TBN, are kind, discreet traveling companions. We have the pleasure of talking in front of the cameras at various times. They ask us to reflect on the existential themes that create a map for exploration to go hand in hand with our pilgrimage. It is like a spiritual schedule, but instead of places, we map universal values to be examined and investigated.

Along this stretch of the road, there are two important themes that guide us through the rolling Tuscan hills heading toward Bagno Vignoni: faith and family. They are particularly close to my heart as I consider them pillars of my life.

Faith, hope, and charity are a triad of Christian theological virtues. But regardless of any religious creed, they are the keys to giving meaning to all our lives and making them complete. They are the foundations of Christian behavior but also universal and interconnected ethical principles. Without hope, we would be trapped in despair. Without faith, life would be a certain tragedy. And without charity, faith and hope could not exist.

Assuming that life on this Earth ends with death—as the ancient saying goes, *nihil morte certius* nothing is more certain than death—our earthly journey would come to a close in certain tragedy. But having no faith, or losing faith, means living in despair.

Faced with difficult situations and the dramas of everyday life, there is no other remedy; no other solution exists. Through faith, pain is almost always eased immediately. But naturally speaking, faith does not come for free. As with any discipline, it requires effort, consistency, and sacrifice. We must acknowledge that our life on Earth is nothing more than a tiny detail in a painting that is infinitely larger than us.

Faith is a gift. It is a beacon, a light to rekindle and enhance humility. If we think we can challenge God's logic, then faith is shattered, and a void is left in its place. We must trust in God's designs, like falling into a father's embrace. I am reminded of Tolstoy's words in *A Confession*: "Whatever answers faith gives, regardless of which faith, or to whom the answers are given, such answers always give an infinite meaning to the finite existence of man; a meaning that is not destroyed by suffering, deprivation, or death.... Faith is the force of life. If a man lives, then he must believe in something. If he did not believe that there was something he must live for, he would not live. If he does not see and comprehend the illusion of the finite, he will believe in the finite. If he does understand the illusion of the finite, he is bound to believe in the infinite. Without faith, it is impossible to live."

Blaise Pascal, a philosopher whose writings I often turn to, describes faith in his Pensées as a wager worth taking: "If you win, you win everything; if you lose, you lose nothing." He suggests skeptics try training for faith, emulating that gift while waiting for it to arrive. This prepares them to embrace it. It is an intriguing paradox of cause and effect, just like the effort to smile we were talking about earlier, an effort that inherently inclines you toward happiness.

As for *family*, there is no society that can do without it, just as there are no houses without bricks. It was the first block laid down by our Creator in building humankind. Family is a necessity and must be defended, protected, and supported. It is the cornerstone of society. It is the ideal place where we seek harmony and mutual respect. Where we are schooled and learn to choose the option that leads to good, putting into practice those Christian values that our parents taught us and that we are responsible for passing down to our children.

Family was (and still is) my rock. There's the family I had the privilege to be born into—my two parents, who taught me about tenacity but also beauty, both internal and external—and then the extended family I created as an adult.

In the early 2000s, due to the complicated situation of my relationships, I almost lost all enthusiasm for my work. My marriage to Veronica played a vital role in finding it again. I might have even given up singing if it had not been for her, my point of reference, my source of serenity and unity.

Toward Bagno Vignoni

We will Traveling approximately 20 miles today, to reach Bagno Vignoni. The journey ends up being more complicated than we expected. For a long stretch, we ride alongside the state highway and cross overpasses and rivers. Then we turn onto a tarmac road that we travel along for a few miles up to our base camp, which we reach, exhausted, after a long uphill stretch.

For lunch, we stop at Gallina, an old farming village. When we get onto a dirt road, I can finally set off at a gallop. Then we arrive at Castiglione d'Orcia, an extremely beautiful medieval village dominated by the Rocca Aldobrandesca, a castle named after the Aldobrandeschi feudal family who built it in the tenth century.

We are forced to dismount here due to the steep, narrow streets paved with old, slippery *Sanpietrini* cobblestones that make our horses struggle to keep their balance. Once we leave the village, we head out into yet another forest where more little pitfalls soon await us. At the end of the path, we come to a ford that has become impassable due to rubble blocking the way. To make our crossing less risky, we are forced to remove as much debris as we can. After a few miles of riding under the shade of the trees, we reach our destination, where our horses can be freed of their saddles and get some much-needed food and water.

"Sacred to nymphs and gods"—this is how Bagno Vignoni is defined in an ancient Roman inscription. Its thermal waters have been popular and cherished for over two millennia. Documents attest to how the thermal springs were regularly open to the public in medieval times. They have even found ancient price lists for entry to the baths and for renting cushions and blankets.

Piazza delle Sorgenti is truly magical, with its enormous pool in the center framed by Renaissance buildings. Steam rises off the water, which reaches almost 120 degrees Fahrenheit. It offers pilgrims precious therapeutic powers with its wealth of salts, calcium, iron carbonate, sodium sulfate, and magnesium.

We take off our boots and enjoy a restorative bath before dinner as a welcome reward for our hard efforts. We are joined for dinner by my two older children, Matteo and Amos. The latter has just finished his day's work in Florence, where he is personally in charge of an Andrea Bocelli Foundation project for the blind. The dinner is even more cheerful with them there.

We finished eating in time to watch an Inter Milan game on TV. I passionately love soccer. Sure, it is just a game, but it excites and moves people, unites and divides them. When you think about it, a pitch is like an opera with an arena of heroes, actors in a dream we chose to live. Acrobats who run around miming battles, expressing creative virtuosity, loving and hating, falling down and getting back up, exposed to the judgment of the spectators in the stands, ever poised between glory and defeat.

My relationship with soccer can be broken down into three stages. I first got into it at boarding school. I was one of the many boys who would walk around with the radio at their ear every Sunday, listening to the minute-by-minute soccer reports. I grew away from it when I was around thirty. I would follow the Sunday games on rare occasions, though remaining fond of Inter Milan, and would cheer on the national team when they played. Then, I went back to soccer when I became a father. I wanted to pass on the values and beauty of the sport to my children, along with the playful passion of supporting a team. To be honest, I wanted everyone in the family to pick the same team. So, I guided them along in order to "affiliate" their soccer allegiances, making sure that none of them became a Juventus supporter!

With Beatrice Venezi

A fellow musician (and fellow Tuscan) with a wonderful character, Beatrice Venezi, joins us on this stretch of the pilgrimage as a traveling and musical companion. Born in 1990, she has achieved a great career and much success even at such a young age. As talented as she is, beautiful, cultured, and charismatic, Beatrice reminds me of Veronica in some ways, kind and strong-willed in equal measures. She is a lovely conversationalist and a meticulous professional with sharp sensitivity and innate leadership skills. Essential qualities for an orchestra conductor. Television audiences recently had a chance to admire her work as a judge and co-conductor at the Sanremo Music Festival. And even in such a tricky role, she was excellent as always.

We got her to conduct at Teatro del Silenzio back in 2019. The energy she transmitted on the stage in Lajatico actively contributed to the show *Ali di libertà*. Then for the huge event held 2022 at Buckingham Palace for Queen Elizabeth's 70th Platinum Jubilee, she stood on the conductor's podium to lead me through "Nessun Dorma" from Puccini's *Turandot*. We have certainly shared great moments together.

That was not the first time I sang in front of Her Majesty. I also took part in the concert for her ninetieth birthday. Throughout the years, I have had the pleasure of meeting and getting acquainted with various members of the royal family. One time, when I was at their residence as a guest, I felt the urge to escape the crowded reception and find a bit of peace and quiet. After setting off down a side corridor, I was literally tackled by security guards. I had been heading right into the queen's private rooms!

I have collected so many stories over my thirty years of performing. They inevitably become top topics of conversation when you find yourself around a big table sharing food with family or a group of old friends. For instance, one of these stories from a life lived was when Veronica and I were invited to a dinner at the White House. The taxi driver got lost in the streets of Washington, making us extremely late. When we finally arrived, it was way past the agreed time. We desperately hoped that we would be able to take our places without being seen. Instead, we found ourselves in front of the president and his wife, who were waiting for us before starting the banquet. Another time, at a dinner at the White House, I grew bothered by the frivolous chatter around me that gave no sign of easing. Seeing my distress, my wife told me that there was a piano in the room. I got up, went over to the piano, and started to play and sing. Immediately, the chatter stopped (and so did the dinner).

Sant'Antimo

Legend has it that Sant'Antimo was founded by none other than Charlemagne. Returning from Rome along the Via Francigena in 781 AD, his army was struck down by a plague. So, the emperor made an offering and promised to build an abbey if the contagion abated. Whether this be truth or legend, the fact is that Sant'Antimo is one of the oldest, most solemn, and most evocative holy places in Italy.

The monastery complex stands majestically amid largely unspoiled countryside. Its gorgeous church is one of the region's most notable and renowned Romanesque monuments. On the southern side, we come to the cloister, a courtyard surrounded by a portico around which the monastery's other buildings were constructed. Matteo and I sit down here. I take up a guitar while he picks up a letter he has written and reads it to me. This is the letter I have included at the start of this book. It contains his profound and moving thoughts written to his father and all our traveling companions.

Inside the church, a chamber orchestra awaits us beneath the wooden crucifix of the main altar. With Beatrice conducting, I sing a short anthology of religious songs. One of these, "Angele Dei" (Angel of God), was composed by Giacomo Puccini while he was studying music in Lucca. It has only been discovered in recent years. It is made up of thirty-one bars with an inspired and softly meditative melody where Puccini's poetic traits and creative sensitivity were already apparent. When I heard the melodic line in the past, I requested that some words of prayer dedicated to the guardian angel be added to it. Then, I performed the song as a worldwide exclusive in San Francisco in 2019.

Our set list also includes a more vivacious score, Gioachino Rossini's "Domine Deus." The virtuosity of this piece proposes a different form of devotion, though it is just as believable and genuine.

Among the Vines

"Life is too short to drink bad wine," as Goethe once said. We are in Montalcino, the land of wine. A name that evokes an exquisitely fine wine made exceptional by its lingering aroma is Brunello. It is funny to think that four hundred years ago, the people of this area used to make white wine, such as Moscadello di Montalcino. In the second half of the nineteenth century, upon his return from fighting for Garibaldi, the winemaker Ferruccio Biondi Santi decided to devote his vineyards to just one grape variety, Sangiovese Grosso. And so the wine-growing history of the area suddenly changed direction.

I love wine. I drink it in moderation, and my preference for Italian wines is no secret. The generosity of our land has never betrayed those who love and respect it. I believe that the quality of our wine has improved a lot in the last quarter of a century, ever since many producers have begun looking at winemaking as an art and a science, both old and modern.

They had always made good wines in the lands where I was born, from Lajatico to Terricciola, long before places like Montalcino and Bolgheri became popular, back when the concept of "green harvesting" would have caused a scandal when grapes were pressed under bare feet, and the harvest was a celebration for everyone.

As for my family's wine, I am too biased to give an opinion. However, I do believe that every good wine—including that produced from our vines—should be natural and sustainable. It should stem from a mutually generous and respectful relationship between the people and the land where they live and work. I enjoy the Bocelli wines, with no exception. My favorite would be Terre di Sandro. This is for rigorously sentimental reasons, as it is named after my beloved father.

Winemaking is a tradition that we are carrying on, mostly thanks to my brother Alberto. For some years now, we have trusted in the support of professionals—essential nowadays—such as agronomists (people in agriculture who deal with crop raising and soil care) and enologists (people who deal with wine and winemaking). Our main priority is for our wines to be ambassadors of the beauty of the Tuscan land and the quality of its fruits.

My father loved the land, just as his father and his father's father before him. My grandfather used to say: "We are poets of the land." As soon as he could, he would leave his store to escape to the paradise of his fields. In those times, every farmer in the area made their own wine. It was the pride and joy of the farm.

Our family has farming origins. In the eighteenth century, my ancestors worked the land owned by the noble Corsini family. In the fifteenth century, those same lands had been among the property of none other than Lorenzo de' Medici, Lorenzo the Magnificent (Italian statesman and patron of artists). Down through the generations, little by little, my ancestors became owners of a small farm. And after overcoming hundreds of problems, the property expanded. My grandfather even managed to give work and homes to a few families under tenant farming.

Even after he opened his new business, my grandfather's love was fully dedicated to the land. My father inherited this passion from him, together with his farming business and a trail of problems. However, he rolled up his sleeves, and with my mother's invaluable help, he kept on going with enthusiasm, ideas, and fresh energy. Together, they succeeded in further expanding the confines and objectives of the property, with special attention to the vines and the wine cellar, a wine cellar where I would often play as a child. I remember walking through it, awed by those huge wooden barrels and earthenware brick vaults.

Just like good music, good wine is one of life's greatest pleasures, providing you have a healthy approach and do not use (or rather abuse) it as did poor Cassio in Shakespeare's Othello!

Opera music and wine are two of the most beloved symbols of Italian excellence throughout the world. Singing arises from a burst of euphoria, and wine inclines the soul towards singing. However, I should specify that when I am preparing to perform on stage, I adhere to an athlete's strict regime. So, my diet does not allow alcohol.

Speaking of stages and wine, I confess that there is one variety that I cannot seem to enjoy, though I understand its value. I am talking about the wine made from the red Lambrusco grape. It was much beloved by my unforgettable friend and musical master, Luciano Pavarotti. One day, he invited me to his villa in Modena. We were sitting in front of an abundant dinner of all kinds of wonders, a table laden with splendid sweet and savory delicacies. Luciano told me to help myself, saying: "Go ahead, tenor. Enjoy." Quite embarrassed, I told him I was on a diet. "Forget about the diet!" he said. "Diets are bad for you. Eat!"

I tasted some food, and he immediately poured me a glass of wine. "Drink this, it's excellent! I know you Tuscans love strong wines, but believe me, this Lambrusco is one of a kind." After tasting the contents of the glass, my parochial spirit and, most of all, my wish to defuse the tension with a funny quip got the better of my good manners. Half serious, I provocatively replied: "Maestro, don't be offended, but this wine is only good for two things: making balsamic vinegar or cleaning mud from the wheels of your car!"

The Castle of Potentino

A different kind of evening awaits us just outside Seggiano at the Castle of Potentino on Mount Amiata. You can feel thousands of years of history in the magnificence of this structure towering above the hills amidst the vineyards. Hearing about its history, we learn how some of the most prominent local families competed for this monumental property in the past.

In the thirteenth century, it was linked to the Aldobrandeschi family, and in the fourteenth century to the Buonsignori, Tolomei, and Salimbeni (with this latter family hosting Saint Catherine within these very walls). Then, in the seventeenth century, the castle was acquired by the Bourbon del Monte, one of the most important aristocratic lineages of the Grand Duchy of Tuscany.

It is currently owned by the descendants of the famous writer Graham Greene. After two decades of renovations, they have transformed it into a cultural and entrepreneurial gem. It hosts academics, wine lovers, artists, volunteers, and all kinds of fascinating people from all over the world.

Upon our arrival, we are greeted by a men's folk choir, who offer us an enjoyable compilation of old Tuscan songs. We are then brought to a room where both Veronica and I are honored with the order of the Grand Cross. Finally, on the ground floor, once more accompanied and entertained by the music of the traditional vocal ensemble, we are presented with a lavish dinner of delicious food and excellent wine. A sweet reprieve from the Spartan pace we had been put through these past few days.

CHAPTER 4

From Buonconvento to Chiusdino

Dolce è Sentire

At 4 a.m., we are already up and about, and one hour later, we are in the saddle. Our early rise regrettably also involves the deputy mayor and the parish priest: one to say goodbye and the other to give us his blessing. The director, Paolo Sodi, finds an iconic location, a perfect framing with an arch of cypress trees against the open backdrop of hills rolling back with the sculptural quality of drapery carved by Michelangelo. His idea is to film me riding along through this magical scene at sunrise, singing *Dolce è Sentire—Fratello Sole, Sorella Luna* a cappella.

The sacrifice will be worth it, though initially, there are various setbacks working against us. First of all, there is an unexpected blanket of fog covering most of the view. We patiently wait for it to clear, and finally, over two hours later, a pallid sun peeps out. We try to film the scene, but toward the end, a man enters the frame, stubbornly determined to continue along his path, indifferent to the staff's pleading. So we have to do it all again. But the location is so beautiful, and the song is so moving that more than one person, including the director himself, sheds a few tears.

I am particularly fond of this prayer in song form. This is also for personal reasons. I am friends with the man who composed the song, Riz Ortolani. I also know Franco Zeffirelli, the director who made the wonderful film of the same name (*Brother Sun, Sister Moon*) about the life of Saint Francis of Assisi.

I once asked myself which contemporary figures could be compared to the great geniuses of the Italian Renaissance. Zeffirelli was first on my list. I have always admired the amount of love this immense artist put into the things he did, his constant and even spasmodic tension regarding beauty, and everything poetic expressed by the world.

Zeffirelli has been an important reference for me throughout my entire existence. As a child, I could feel the echo of his directorial creations and the amazing synergy he created in melodrama. As a teenager, I could feel the power of love in *Romeo and Juliet*. As an eighteen-year-old, I was deeply moved by his masterpiece Jesus of Nazareth. I could go on for every era of my life. An immense devotion to opera and its great creators were the building blocks for the solid friendship we created over the years, bolstered by the respect and gratitude I have always felt for his art. As he was one of the great leading players in the golden age of opera, I never tired of talking to and asking him about it. Each time, it was patently clear to me how privileged I was to have him beside me.

I was asked to take part in the 2009 documentary *Omaggio a Roma*, directed by Zeffirelli. I was initially flattered and amused, but then I started to get worried. Though aware of my acting limitations, I could not miss such a once-in-a-lifetime opportunity. I had no doubt in my mind. So, with a good dose of recklessness, I immediately replied: "Count me in whenever and however you need me.""

On set, he was a kind, friendly, even thoughtful guide. He was very patient, and I think in the end, he was happy with what I managed to do with my best efforts. The film script based on the three-act opera Tosca by Puccini included a slightly racy scene between Monica Bellucci and me. For my love of art, shall we put it, I willingly stepped forward to act out a passionate kiss (imitating the sensual ardor between Cavaradossi and Floria Tosca), but my wife's presence meant I could not fully engage with the scene. So, Franco advised Veronica to step off the set for a moment for the good of the artistic outcome (also to spare her suffering). And with her customary intelligence and class, Veronica accepted Zeffirelli's advice.

In more recent years, I was asked to inaugurate his foundation. Later, we also celebrated together the lucky coincidence of both of our foundations, his nonprofit Franco Zeffirelli Foundation and the Andrea Bocelli Foundation, opening their offices in the same building in Florence. I was very saddened to hear of his passing in 2019. I regret that I never got to do the *Bohème*, an opera in three acts by Puccini, that he was so keen to make with me at the theater and then on film. He was passionate about the project, but his time ran out in the end.

The Poor Man of Assisi

I had the honor of singing *Fratello Sole Sorella Luna* in front of Pope Benedict XVI and hundreds of thousands of young people in Loreto in 2007. Ten years later, I sang it once more for Pope Francis and again on the stage of Teatro del Silenzio together with my son Matteo. Singing it again this morning, astride my horse in a poetic, esoteric setting, is a powerful experience. With its simple melody, the song is about life and all of us. It evokes the wonder of creation, recalling the themes of a song— "Canticle of the Sun"—composed by the saint and poet Saint Francis of Assisi in 1224.

The world is currently going through an extremely tough time with huge international tensions, unprecedented economic issues, and violent friction between different religions and cultures intent on destroying adversaries, antagonists, and anyone who is different rather than making an effort to build what is an essential condition for the harmonious and safe growth of humanity as a whole: *dialogue*.

When I think about Francis of Assisi and try to imagine him immersed in his everyday life, entirely focused on investigating the mystery and meaning of life in greater depth, I find myself looking at a man open to dialogue like no other—open to dialogue with nature, with animals, and, above all, with other people. Francis was probably a man of few words: "Let your 'Yes' mean 'Yes,' and your 'No' mean 'No.'" (Matthew 5:37.) And, to the same degree, he was probably eager to approach others in the most in-depth and brightest example of dialogue, which is listening, understanding, looking the other person in the eye, sparkling with the power of good.

By putting themselves in the place of God, people are even more alone. Blinded by contagious egoism, they labor to accumulate riches, becoming poorer as they go. They learn foreign languages, and they speak with ever greater command of speech while understanding each other less and less. They pray to the same God and fight about which is the right way to do so. They say one thing, do another, and think something else altogether.

But the "poor man of Assisi" is still among us. His life, the example he set, and his silent lesson still have the same effect on our innermost conscience, shaking it hard, to the point of making it uncomfortable and unpleasant for us, as only the truth can be.

Francis of Assisi stands out and dominates the hearts of everyone who stops to listen. Everything becomes clear in just a few moments, illuminated by an idea that does not fear the passage of time and the rapid changing of customs and promises us serenity and peace, which are not long in coming.

There is no growth without dialogue, and, as a result, there is no hope. Dialogue between different religions is much desired. To achieve this, people need to find the strength and humility to finally replace their ego with God. The cause of all human tragedies, with no exception, can be found right there in that small insignificant word that fills our mouths every day: *I*. "I have the right; I know the truth of everything; I can; I come first because I am the god that you must worship."

Good Lord! Once more, I was the one doing the talking, as if I had the right to do so. But now I will be quiet so that you can talk to me through the poor, the sick, the least fortunate. And from their lips, words of truth and life reach my heart.

The Last Goddess

There was a particularly lovely legend told by the Greek poet Hesiod in the seventh century BC. Hope, personified in Elpis, is the only item that remains in Pandora's box after all the others fly away. This is where we get the Latin saying *Spes ultima dea*—hope, the last goddess.

Now more than ever, *hope* is what can tip the existential scales. Without it, we are trapped in despair. If we have no hope, fear creeps in. And, as some would say, fear is the only thing we should fear. The challenge is to keep our nerve and not lose our serenity, optimism, and confidence in the future, avoiding the needless waste of energy and immune defenses that cause panic and stress. Natural disasters, pandemics, wars. History has taught us that even larger stumbling blocks have been overcome in the past, at times with surprising speed. In my opinion, being optimistic is a moral duty.

Those who hold and safeguard hope in their heart are fulfilled. Those who lose hope fall into despair, the worst of all evils. It follows to conclude that those who sow hope do good, while those who sow despair do evil. Those who inspire others to have faith create lasting hope, hope that makes people happy. Those who inspire others to atheism take away hope, thus generating unhappiness.

The trials we have endured since 2020 have torn a universal wound that will scar us for a long time. But the world needs to get back to designing, creating culture, and spending time with art to find faith, hope, and even our own identities once again. This is the message I want to transmit through song.

Like almost everyone, my life has not been lacking in slumps and times of difficulty. But as my life story has been an adventure with a happy ending in a certain sense, I hope it can act as a useful testimony to the message it conveys. The message is that there is no such thing as an impossible dream. The important thing is to believe in your dream and pursue it with honesty, reliability, and humility without ever falling into despair.

Any kind of self-pity is so counterproductive! Yet, all of us can see it in our lives. Instead, we should always think of life in constructive and optimistic terms, focusing on how to best explore and spend our lives. Finding a career in music for a country boy like me, without any contacts in the entertainment industry, was an audacious challenge. Achieving success was far from certain. That is why my father insisted I also go to college. However, I never gave up on the hope of being able to make a living and support a family through music, even while I was studying law and playing in piano bars.

For the first thirty-five years of my life, a career in music remained a fantasy, something I had glimpsed but never attained. I came up against many closed doors. I worked my way up, encountering a lot of setbacks and barely missed opportunities. Many important people from show business advised me to change careers.

During those moments, when there were so few people willing to bet on me, my great allies were hope (to improve, to be respected and understood), confidence in my passion, my obstinacy, and my desire to make the most out of any mishaps along the way and anything that could have been done differently and better. Even back then, just as now, I fought every day to live in light and only in light, keeping the shadows at bay at all costs.

I am reminded of a beautiful old song by Grammy-award-winning singer and later an Italian politician Domenico Modugno:, "Meraviglioso." In the verses of that song, an angel dressed as a passerby reminds us of the power of hope and beauty in the world with heartrending simplicity. True beauty is always innate to goodness.

Tori Kelly

Our journey has another Tuscan gem in store for us in the heart of the lunar landscape of Crete Senesi. Buonconvento is a medieval village surrounded and protected by its famous red walls dating back to the fourteenth century. Our traveling companion for a stretch of road today is Tori Kelly.

She rides a quarter horse with a western saddle that Pasquale, my friend, prepared for her. Tori is a young twenty-eight-year-old Californian singer who is very famous in the US, where she was born to parents of Jamaican, Puerto Rican, Irish, and German ancestry. With this jumble of cultures and musical influences mixed with her Christian upbringing, she developed a passion for singing at a young age. She used to take part in important television contests, winning *America's Most Talented Kid* when she was eleven. But her early successes also brought her some disappointments. She had to face stinging rejection as a teenager.

However, Tori is now one of the US's most highly respected young artists. Her second studio album, *Hiding Place* (2018), got to 35 on the Billboard 200 chart and won two Grammy Awards for best gospel album and best gospel song.

While the clouds over our heads swell with threats of rain, we ride along, having a pleasant chat about our experiences of life, music, and faith. Veronica jokingly points out how my English becomes more confident and fluent in the presence of a beautiful woman. We have found a lovely harmony that will soon resonate when we sing together at our next stop. Tori tells us about her experience with failure and how much her faith helped and supported her when the world suddenly seemed to have forgotten her. Paradoxically, her darkest moments gave her the strength to head in new directions, perfect her voice, learn to play the guitar, and compose some new songs herself.

It is refreshing to hear the story of this young artist who perfectly embodies that winning attitude that I always advise the new generations to adopt. Never accept defeat; never stop believing in your own potential. Do not complain, but instead react with determination and faith in your passion, keeping in mind that success, if and when it comes, is triggered by unfathomable variables.

It must also be pointed out that fame, in and of itself, is not a value at all. It is enjoyable and flattering, but it does not actually lead to anything. It is not a quality. In fact, there are thousands of ways of being a person of great value without being famous. That being said, there is nothing wrong with aspiring to success. But standing out from the crowd has always been hard, and it always will be. In order to try, you must arm yourself with a strong will and spirit of sacrifice. Otherwise, you will not get anywhere. You also need to cultivate your talent and hope that your destiny holds a chance for others to discover the service you offer society with your art.

When the show business spotlight moved away from Tori Kelly around ten years ago, she did not give up. She produced and recorded an EP, *Handmade Songs*, by herself in her bedroom. The album ended up in the iTunes Top 10.

Mentors

I believe in guardian angels. I believe we all have a heavenly protector watching over our journey on Earth. More prosaically, I also believe in the possibility of bumping into, or even attracting, flesh-and-bone angels on our path, people who can make a difference in our lives. I use a word that is a bit archaic in Italian—mentor—but which I am fond of because it increases the potential of every life as it blossoms. We also talked about this with Tori Kelly. It is the art of learning how to recognize your teachers and prepare your soul to embrace the positive examples that life offers you.

The term *mentor* comes from Greek mythology. In Homer's Odyssey, Odysseus placed Mentor in charge of his beloved son Telemachus before leaving for the Trojan War. This shows us the meaning and value of an archetype that is vital for the evolution of humanity and, thus, each one of us.

Before I embarked on my international career, there were very few people who believed in my dreams or encouraged my professional ambitions—except for the constant support of my parents because mothers and fathers are mentors of the highest quality. However, I had the privilege of finding two people along my journey who embody the term *mentor* perfectly.

The first was Amos Martellacci from my hometown. I owe much of what I know to him. Amos was an extraordinary man who could speak six languages and became a bank manager even though he never completed high school. God gave him the gift of an extraordinary ability to learn and understand, along with the irrepressible desire to transmit something of himself to others. He found me on his path. He made the sacrifice of coming to my house every morning and evening for many years, helping me with my college studies until my music career took off. I named my firstborn son Amos in his honor.

Another great encounter came both before and after Amos. I heard his voice as a child and then had the privilege of having him as a teacher and friend as an adult—Franco Corelli, one of history's greatest tenors.

I was eight when I first had the uplifting experience of hearing the voice and, I wish to add, the soul of this unique singer. My nanny, Oriana, had told me about him with great enthusiasm, though she was perhaps attracted more to the physical appearance of the great singer than his objective vocal qualities. I badgered my mother and father until they bought me one of Corelli's singles on vinyl. The A-side had "Improvviso" from Umberto Giordano's opera *Andrea Chénier*.

With a child's typical impatience, I ran straight to the old record player. I turned it on, starting the platter by pushing out the tonearm and delicately placing it on the new 45 rpm vinyl. The record player introduced me to the music of that great story. Finally, a voice filled the breaks of the orchestra and reached my ears. I heard the words *"Colpito qui m'avete"* through a voice that was completely different from all the others, a long, vibrating voice brimming with emotion, filled with indefinable suffering, that went straight to my heart. The singing was loose, free, spontaneous, sometimes sweet, sometimes roaring, but always authoritative and dominating.

"Improvviso" is a poetic, moving song, but it needs a singer who can identify with a character like Chénier, a poet whose drama is played out in the complex world of the French Revolution. The vocal line must be elegant but convincing and decisive at the same time. Chénier tackles the theme of intense love in a broad sense. Corelli, on the other hand, seemed to be tackling the theme of love for his own art: the art of singing, which can captivate, move, and transform a spirit hardened by the trials of life.

Oriana and I listened, won over by a new, incredible bliss. At one stage, I saw my nanny put her hands over her eyes while the tenor, with an incomparable sweetness, began to sing: *"Oh, giovinetta bella, d'un poeta non disprezzate il detto: Udite! Non conoscete amor"* (Oh beautiful young lady, don't discredit the words of a poet. Listen! You don't know love). That day marked my destiny. His voice had fatefully touched my heart and ignited my imagination. He freed something that would perhaps have remained imprisoned in a simple soul forever had I not listened to that record. I loved that tenor from the very first time I listened to him. As a young man, I consumed his records. Still, later, I had the immense privilege of studying with him, forming a relationship of mutual respect and genuine devotion.

San Galgano

The milky pockets of clouds finally decide to release their water down to wet the earth. It starts raining and goes on to rain all day long. We stop for a few minutes to shelter in a barn, hoping that the sky will clear, but we realize that we will just have to brave it out and keep going. Half an hour later, we say goodbye to our kind guest, Tori, which means we can pick up the pace.

We set off again under the unrelenting rain that does not give us a moment's reprieve. Luckily, the road presents no obstacles, and we can continue along at pace despite the slippery, wet terrain.

Even this kind of day is a gift, a powerful experience. Rain is usually something we try to dodge. This goes for everyone and even more for those like me whose work depends on always being in perfect health. As a matter of fact, I cannot remember a day like that when I spent hours in the rain, at least not as an adult. Experiencing that sensation once again, aside from the discomfort of drenched clothes, creates a feeling of harmony with nature that is hard to describe. The rain never stopped the pilgrims.

After hours on the road, soaking wet and starving, we dismount our horses and eat some focaccia and pasta we buy in a bakery we find. And finally, after some detours for technical reasons and a well-earned night of rest, we arrive at the Abbey of San Galgano.

Bundling the Eremo di Montesiepi and the thirteenth-century church in the form of a Latin cross, the complex sits in a grassy valley between the hills of Chiusdino, around twenty miles from Siena. The abbey symbolizes a huge wound for Christianity. Its lacerations have given it an evocative power that makes it truly unique. Its roof is the sky, and the sky also fills the rose window and the two single light, narrow, arched monofora windows of the apse.

San Galgano was deconsecrated in the eighteenth century following its deterioration due to pestilence, lightning, and various raids (the lead roof was sold to make bullets). Inspired by Cistercian Gothic architecture, the surviving structure still today imbues pilgrims with its holy energy and mystical nature as a corridor between heaven and earth.

Canonized in 1185, Galgano Guidotti was a medieval knight who became a hermit. This famous abbey was devoted to him, as was the nearby monastery and Romanesque-style chapel. Still today, you can see the sword that the saint is said to have stuck into the stone in order to transform it into a Christian symbol. Indeed, there is a fascinating theory that it was not Tuscany that imitated the Breton Round Table legend but rather the other way round. The theory also hypothesizes that the story of the Grail could be a Persian readaptation of the story of the three wise men, which reached Europe around the eleventh century, colored by its passage through Italy with the figure of Galgano (renamed Perceval) and then developed by Chrétien de Troyes at the court of Aquitaine.

A Common Language

The rain has made the air crystal clear and fresh with a slight bite to it. The sky over the abbey offers an uneven veil of high and almost transparent cirrus clouds. This is a rest day for our horses and also for us, but in a different way. We will regain our strength through music.

It is a privilege to let my voice reverberate in such a magnificent setting, surrounded by a rolling landscape with the rhythm of a slow waltz, moving through vines and olive trees, oaks, chestnuts, holly oaks, firs, hedges, and aromatic herbs. A truly holy land, packed with churches dating back thousands of years, farms, castles, and fortifications that have cast off the poison of their aggression. They are now sweetened with fairy tales and old legends.

A cheerful atmosphere infects the entire group, from the artists and technicians to the US film crew. So many people have turned up to play and sing together. We meet Tori Kelly again, along with the 40 Fingers guitar quartet and the Sisters and Brothers Gospel Choir Ensemble. We are also joined by 2Cellos, the cello duo Luka Šulić and Stjepan Hauser. I have invited these talented young musicians to important events in the past, including the philanthropic concert at the Colosseum for the Celebrity Fight Night in Italy in 2017, along with Steven Tyler, Elton John, and many others.

The universal language of music joins and unites this unique international lineup gathered together in the heart of Tuscany within the walls of this holy place. The empathy and harmony that spring forth are reflected in the quality of the recordings and the beauty of the songs we sing for the TBN cameras without even rehearsing them.

Tori's voice interweaves with mine in our rendering of Leonard Cohen's "Hallelujah." I am particularly fond of this song as it was the first duet I ever sang with my daughter, Virginia. It is not strictly a religious song, but it is permeated with deep reverence. A true ode to life. We partially adapted the lyrics to make it suitable for a child's voice. The new version, created for my album *Believe*, respects the atmosphere and colors created by the Canadian musician and poet while taking the gamble of performing it as a duet, doubling the main voices and also the lyrics in two languages, English and Italian.

More emotions under the sky and within the walls of San Galgano. More music with the gospel group, the four guitarists, the cello players, and Tori's magical voice. The songs she performs include a moving version of "Amazing Grace," a classic of global musical tradition. Inspired by a conversion and conceived in the eighteenth century, the power of this Christian hymn still moves and touches us today. The lyrics were written by the London native John Newton, who had previously been the captain of slave ships. After repenting and converting to Christianity, he became the parish priest of Olney. He had the following words engraved on his tomb: "John Newton. Clerk. Once an infidel and libertine, a servant of slaves in Africa, was by the rich mercy of our Lord and Saviour Jesus Christ preserved, restored, pardoned, and appointed to preach the faith he had long labored to destroy."

I get the 2Cellos to accompany me on another song that unites and warms the hearts of big crowds—"You'll Never Walk Alone," a declaration of love and common solidarity that restores the certainty of a "golden sky" after a storm. An extremely successful song, it started its life on Broadway in 1945 and then became a standard song for graduation parties as well as one of the most beloved hymns in the history of sport in the UK.

An Angel with Boxing Gloves

The morning performance ends with a group lunch at a restaurant just a few minutes walk from San Galgano.

Music prepares us for the pleasure of conversation and reflection. Chatting with our dining companions, alternating between Italian and English, we return to the topics of *hope, faith,* and *mentors*: those reference figures in music and beyond, those "champions" that inspire and guide us with the tangible example of their lives and actions.

I automatically think of a great man, a universal icon of bravery and civil commitment: Muhammad Ali, one of the most important figures of our lifetime.

Some years ago, I was fortunate enough to meet him and even become his friend after a lifetime of watching him in the ring with great passion and admiration. Meeting him was a dream come true. I was brought to his home as an unexpected guest by our mutual friend Jimmy Walker, who had been invited there for Muhammad Ali's wife Lonnie's birthday.

When I found that immense athlete before me, a man exhausted but not bowed by illness, Ali broke a silence that apparently had lasted days, to the amazement and emotion of those present, saying to me in a barely audible voice: "Sing for me." I fell to my knees and, with great joy, honored his request, dedicating an Italian melody to him a cappella, my voice cracking with emotion. That day, Muhammad gave me two signed boxing gloves, which I keep as a memento at home in the room that I often use for recording.

The next day, at the Phoenix Arena filled with spectators, Muhammad Ali was in the front row. I went on stage wearing his gloves and celebrated him on the final notes of "Nessun Dorma." There could be no better words to greet a great warrior, I thought than those final lyrics repeated three times: "*vincerò*" (I will win), perfect for expressing a frame of mind distinguished by burning passion and boundless willpower, just like the invincible champion there before me.

"The man with no imagination has no wings," Muhammad Ali once said. In the end, he truly learned to fly, transcending a body that had first brought him triumph and then imprisoned him. But he never stopped fighting the illness that afflicted him. In the last thirty years of his life, he was never alone in the ring. Alongside him was his soulmate, his beloved Lonnie, with him to the last. They took on the battle against Parkinson's together as a couple.

Celebrating the memory of Muhammad Ali, a hero who never disappointed, an example in his sport, and in his extraordinary civil commitment, we implicitly celebrate his wonderful wife Yolanda (Lonnie), "the boss" as he affectionately called her, his guardian angel.

When Muhammad passed away, by sheer coincidence, I was on stage in San Jose, California, just a two-hour flight away from him. I knew that his illness had advanced and that he had been taken to the hospital. In my heart, however, I kept hoping against hope that the "greatest" would once again knock out that illness, his most persistent opponent. Once I heard the news, I decided to dedicate *Con te partirò* to him. I told the audience how I liked the idea of Muhammad up there in heaven, generous and strong, still fighting for a better world as he always had.

His ideals, his values, and the battles that he fought are still alive and strong as ever. The best way to commemorate him is to follow in his footsteps.

CHAPTER 5

From San Rocco to Pilli to San Gimignano

Siena and Its Heroes

I love Siena, its perfect architecture, its intense Palio horse race, and the silently magnificent countryside surrounding the city. This is where we plan to set up our base camp, the logistics center for this stretch of the journey. After setting out once more on our pilgrimage from San Galgano, we are going to spend the night in Siena. Along the way, we stop off at San Rocco a Pilli. Then, on this warm sunny day, we continue to Pian del Lago, where our horses—especially Badillon, who seems to be suffering from back pain—enjoy a quick, well-earned rest. We are approached here by an elderly man carrying a wooden crate full of homing pigeons. He shows them to us, talking to us at length about his passion for these wonderful birds and how they are trained to return home. He insists that we try first-hand the thrill of throwing them up into flight.

When we reach Siena, we walk to Piazza del Campo, the symbolic center of the medieval settlement and shell-shaped heart of city life for over seven hundred years, sloping toward the thirteenth-century Palazzo Pubblico with its famous bell tower Torre del Mangia.

We have with us Virginia's young American nanny, Kate. I remember that when she was offered the job, she had no idea who I was. Telling her mother about this job offer in Italy, she asked her if she had, by any chance, heard of a singer called Andrea Bocelli. Dumbfounded, her mother replied: "Are you serious? Everyone has heard of him!"

Once in Italy, she had a chance to see and understand the amount of affection and attention I am kindly given by so many people. However, she did not think I was that famous among her peers.

Indeed, Kate is surprised here in Siena when I am literally mobbed by a crowd of young people her age, looking for a handshake or a selfie. We sit at a table at one of the cafes, looking out onto the square, taking in its splendor. We sip coffee and taste a typical Siena dessert that blends marzipan with vanilla and candied orange peel. This is the exact spot where, twice a year, the cobblestones are covered with a blanket of earth to transform into a racecourse. It is the setting for a wild horse race with bareback riders along the outer ring of the square.

The Palio di Siena is famous and beloved all over the world. Merging the sacred and the profane, this competition (definitely not a commemoration!) sees ten participants compete from ten *contrade*, or city wards, chosen at random from among the seventeen that comprise the districts within the city's medieval walls. The goal is to win the banner known as the cencio, a piece of silk of seemingly modest value, but that is actually priceless. Everyone in Siena yearns to have it, anxiously waiting for this race all year long—this serious race comprising three laps galloped around Piazza del Campo.

Siena has been dear to my heart since I was a child. This is partly due to my passion for melodrama and the golden age of its actors. Siena is the native city of the great baritone Ettore Bastianini, a formidable singer whom I have always loved. He was gifted with a "bronze and velvet" timbre, as his many admirers put it. Apart from his amazing performances alongside Maria Callas, Giacomo Lauri-Volpi, and Jussi Björling, I was struck by the story of his brief, intense life.

Born in 1922, he grew up in poverty and without a father. He ignited his astonishing voice thanks to the teachings of Luciano Bettarini, who would also be my first singing teacher years later. When he was just forty years old, Bastianini discovered he had a throat tumor right at the peak of his career. However, he hid the diagnosis, even from his companion. In fact, he left her to spare her the ordeal he was about to face. He refused surgery and continued to sing in theaters, growing increasingly exhausted from the pain and the medicine he was taking.

Captain of the Pantera Contrada, he managed to celebrate victory at the Palio in 1963. He died four years later, and the entire city came out for his funeral. When the funeral procession passed in front of Piazza del Campo, the coffin was turned toward Torre del Mangia while the bell tolled in his honor.

Facing Fear

Fear is a waste of time, and yet we have to face it. We reflect on fear and how to overcome it with our guests and companions on this portion of the pilgrimage.

Both faith and fear require you to believe in something that you cannot see. When we choose to believe that God is with us and loves us, fear instantly loses its power. Fear is a poison; hope is its antidote, and prayer is its antithesis.

Its antidote is any kind of leap toward beauty and thus toward goodness, which, as I never tire of repeating, is linked to true beauty. All kinds of art help, including the art of living and spending your days poetically in harmony with those around you.

Thanks to music, I have always received much more than I have given. However, this does not mean that I have not experienced difficult times. I have often stumbled along the way and then struggled with the extreme effort of pulling myself back up again. In these moments, I have felt firsthand that fear and negativity do not get you anywhere. Negativity is a dependency that—as a priest once said—makes us strangers in life, falsifying everything that is real.

Whenever I have been afraid, I have either overcome it or, failing that, had to miss out on opportunities. Not being afraid means rationalizing the risk and comparing it to the goal we have set ourselves. Fear is a fog that distorts every shape. If you cannot get free of it, unfortunately, you are stuck.

In our everyday lives, we are absorbed by so many distractions and apparent priorities. The ensuing risk is that converging with our soul can be systematically pushed back. Always busy, always competitive, our ego seems invincible (even though it is actually terrified, especially by its own limits).

Our soul, on the other hand, if examined properly—including through music and prayer—can give us different and more in-depth answers. Our soul is in contact with the eternal dimension of time, so it is not afraid of anything. And it reminds us of the beauty and fullness of life, of this earthly journey that perhaps was conceived precisely to make us understand these things, preparing us for what will come after.

Evenings on the Town

Every crisis—whose etymology is linked to "distinguishing" or "choosing"—is also a challenge and an opportunity, as well as a great responsibility. It is useless to be afraid of it, yet young people especially often prefer not to think. They dull their senses with noise, alcohol, and psychoactive drugs, thus renouncing the pleasure of imagining and creating. In truth, they do not want to think about the future because they are afraid. And they fear the future because they do not have the tools needed to face it: values, knowledge, the spirit of sacrifice. They are not at peace with their own conscience and seek escape routes from reality. And when this escape is not enough, indifferent to the irreversible damage that certain experiences can cause, they accept living in modified states of consciousness, as if, at the other end of these absurd trips, they will not have to face reality again, as if they had left it forever.

The contemporary world is complex and full of painful wounds and unsolved problems that have a devastating effect on weaker individuals. Alas, no one has a remedy for them. However, while this can be explained—though not quite justified—for young people, it is much more difficult to understand the behavior of adults who love meeting up for dinner in prestigious locations and spending all evening and night stupefied by alcohol and the booming noise of chart music that forces dining companions to shout to be heard by the person next to them.

As I have sometimes found myself roped into some unfortunate situations like this, I have tried to give meaning to the experience, attempting to find a plausible explanation. The beauty, enjoyment, and meaning of an evening with friends are found in the pleasure of lively, intelligent conversations that lead to stimuli, ideas, plans, hopes, all things that presumably require us to want to give something to those listening and receive something from those talking, something that is worth our time, our attention.

So why should someone be satisfied with creating a situation that prevents any form of dialogue and, thus, spiritual betterment? Because, basically, they have nothing to say and do not have the slightest interest in what others might have to say to them.

This is a very sad situation. Representatives of high society, industrialists, important businesspeople, and leading figures in finance, fashion, etc., are so engrossed in their own personal and work matters that they slowly lose any grasp or awareness of the world around them—a world that they naively believe they can dominate, in a battle of cash and being seen in the right places or meeting the right people, who are obviously the people who matter.

What do they say to each other, though? What can they possibly tell each other? How can they involve those present with matters solely related to the specific sector where they work? This is the problem. The solution is what anyone can experience by attending any one of these social occasions. If they have any common sense, they will leave incredulous and dismayed.

In those places full of well-dressed people, weighed down with jewels and irritatingly curated, often reshaped by plastic surgeons in a vain attempt to eliminate the signs of aging and natural imperfections, you often witness a sort of individual and collective alienation. It leaves you powerless and bewildered. When I manage to get away and recover control of my senses, I confess that I automatically echo whoever came up with that brilliant phrase many centuries ago: "O, happy solitude! O, only happiness!"

Ramin Bahrami

We arrive at Monteriggioni, a walled town that stands over the Via Francigena and overlooks the valleys of Val d'Elsa and Val Staggia. Encircled by walls, its town center is "crowned with towers," as described by Dante Alighieri. Here, just a few feet from the church of Santa Maria Assunta built in the early thirteenth century, along with the surrounding town, we meet the Iranian pianist Ramin Bahrami.

Surrounded by centuries-old olive trees, a grand piano stands out against the green grass and the ancient stones in the background. I give it a try, relying on the patience of the great performer. Ramin is one of the world's most highly esteemed interpreters of Bach's work, and I am delighted to get to talk and sing with him.

According to the charismatic pianist, born in Tehran in 1976 and now living in Germany, "Bach writes for the universe, not just for his fellow creatures. With his timeless music, he can even reach the hearts of children and adolescents. I understood him for the first time when I was four years old, and I felt like his music was coming from heaven."

Charmed by his kind, serene manner and an old-style elegance and civility, Veronica and I feel immediate affection and respect for him. We listen to his extremely moving interpretation of the *Goldberg Variations*, the first great work to come out of Bach's extremely creative period. Composed between 1741 and 1742, they were made in a cosmic balance between music and mathematics, adhering to an extremely strict structure with polyphonic abundance and a pure vocal line.

The Iranian pianist explains to us that, though Bach had never been to Italy, "he was aware of Italy's immense musical culture and had the gift of being able to absorb a country's secrets, becoming more Italian than Italians themselves." Ramin Bahrami also left a piece of his heart in Italy. He first landed here over thirty-five years ago as a refugee fleeing war and persecution. He is always happy to come back to Italy, and he is particularly beloved here. A son of Islam, he trained in music at the Conservatory of Milan under the direction of Piero Rattalino.

His sensitivity has been sharpened by suffering and hardship. Grandson of the first Persian archaeologist to graduate from the Sorbonne, a university in Paris, France, and son of a famous engineer who designed schools and universities for the shah, Ramin was from an early age subject to the violent confiscations following the rise of the fundamentalist regime. His father was locked up for years in the prison of Ayatollah Khomeini and died a prisoner there in 1991, officially due to "cardiac arrest," but he was actually executed. "I was already living in Italy when I heard the news. Those experiences scarred me. They intensified my nostalgic side and made me reflect at length on what really matters," the pianist remembers.

Bahrami managed to declare war on war and overcome fear through music. As a child, he would react to the bombs by putting on records by Russian-born American violinist Jascha Heifetz and pretending to conduct what he was listening to. Thanks to music, he never stops honoring the memory of his father, Paviz, who wrote to him from prison: "Bach will never leave you alone; he will be your guide where I can no longer be."

We say goodbye to Ramin, thanking him with all our hearts. Getting to talk and play music with this immense Persian artist and intellectual was a fascinating experience with Ramin accompanying me on the piano, singing a prayer in song form (Schubert's "Ave Maria"), confirmed to me yet again how God can be called in many ways. He exists and is invoked wherever there is goodness, wherever love is called forth (love is the most pertinent alternative word for our Creator).

These valleys and hills seem truly filled with signs of love. They regale us with sights that many city-dwellers have already forgotten—fields thick with poppies like colonies of red butterflies and, in the evenings, the flickering, dancing magic of fireflies.

Laura Biancalani

Not far from Monteriggioni, another rendezvous awaits us, this time with two dear old friends. We have arranged to meet them at Abbadia Isola. Among the thousand-year-old stones of this strategic site since Etruscan times, alongside the abbey founded in 1001, we dismount our horses and embrace Laura Biancalani, the president of the Andrea Bocelli Foundation, and the priest Marco Casalini.

We soon forget about the cameras filming us and rekindle our customary familiarity and empathy. We sit down on a bench alongside the pilgrim welcome center and reminisce about that day almost thirty years ago when two young people knocked on my door at Poggioncino.

Laura was eighteen, as was her friend Marco. They both had a passion for opera music. She was studying singing and planning to become a lawyer, and he was an organ player. They often played as a duo, singing and playing at weddings to scrape together some money. They were also both focusing on their unbridled vocation to improve the quality of life of others.

At that time, there was a stigma around AIDS. With unpardonable ignorance, people believed that the disease only struck disreputable people. There was so little information. Fear stirred up a discriminatory and irrational phobia in people. Young people were dying in the streets, isolated and destitute. Laura and Marco gave their time as volunteers to help people who had contracted the disease. They had come to me because they were planning a training course for health workers that would end with a fund-raising concert. There were so many victims of that awful disease that they were struggling to even find the money to buy coffins.

I welcomed the two of them into my house. But I had a previous appointment at the Verdi Theatre in Pisa, so I had very little time to give them that day. I asked them to return the next day to explain everything about their work and their request. They came back, and I discovered how much passion lay behind their wish to do all they could for others. I could not fathom how two teenagers could be so sensitive and generous but also determined enough to come knocking on my door with great initiative and spontaneity, asking me to hold a concert in Empoli for their cause. I certainly sensed the authenticity of their reasons, but also a strong empathy and a clear sharing of values. Our inner strings were vibrating in the same direction. So I said to them: "I accept. Count me in."

Over the subsequent months, Laura went knocking on the doors of the public administrations and parishes all over the area. She brought her own savings book around with her, which had a total amount of 700,000 lira (just over 370 US dollars) and would say: "This is the money I have. If you support me, I can promote the concert on a broader scale. The more you help me, the more funds I will have to organize this training in aid of a cause that I consider just."

Many did not believe that I was involved. In fact, I had to do a radio interview to confirm that I would be attending the concert. After that, the tickets were immediately snapped up.

My friendship with Laura and Marco gradually grew. The same thing happened with Veronica (so much so that Laura would become Virginia's godmother). Strengthened by our shared ethics, inner world, and heart, we saw each other grow along our journey. I watched their vocations blossom; they watched my children grow up.

In the meantime, after finishing her law degree, Laura won a scholarship for a master's in management of cooperatives and nonprofits at the Bocconi University School of Management in Milan. Subsequently, she became head of institutional activities and legal affairs of the Cassa di Risparmio di San Miniato Foundation and a member of the National Microcredit Commission of the trade association of foundations and savings banks. In this role, she worked in Italy and abroad, for example, in Bethlehem and Jerusalem, contributing to the development of many small enterprises.

Marco had initially begun studying humanities but soon realized that his vocation lay in another direction. So, after finishing his nurse training studies, he entered the seminary for the priesthood.

Veronica and I met Laura one day and told her about our idea to set up a foundation. This was followed by months of reflection to figure out the vision and mission and study the past in order to better understand the future direction. In July 2011, one week before cementing the establishment of the Andrea Bocelli Foundation with a public notary, I told Laura that I would like to appoint her chairperson of the board. At the end of the year, we presented the foundation in Los Angeles, where many generous, wealthy people could help get this brash but exciting project off the ground.

The foundation grew over the years. When we felt it needed a more solid structure, we asked the engineer and manager Stefano Aversa to be chairman of the board, and we asked Laura to dedicate her time to the foundation full-time, taking on the role of president. Within twenty-four hours, she made the difficult and brave decision to leave her previous job and fully take on this adventure.

In its first eleven years, the foundation raised over forty-three million dollars. These funds are used for schools, food, medicine, and drinking water. Aid is also provided in far-off suffering countries such as Haiti, also closer to home when earthquakes have hit Italian regions, the Marche in particular.

We have also faced cultural challenges in developing talent, in using innovative didactic means, and in spreading languages such as music, art, and digital media at schools. We wage open war on bureaucracy. Our goal is that red tape can be overcome everywhere and all the time in order to let people work on their real, tangible needs.

Spreading Love Throughout the World

Here we are now, sitting on a bench in the Siena countryside, reminiscing about the past, joking about the present, and thinking about all the many projects that the foundation plans to undertake. Four friends linked by one invisible, indestructible common thread. Veronica and Laura work together in harmony and with passion on the many fronts where the foundation is involved. Marco is very active in helping children and teenagers. He also teaches religions at professional institutes located in multi-ethnic and sometimes disadvantaged areas. His students were some of the first to join the ABF GlobaLAB, a strategic professional project that aims to incentivize and guide the talents of the future.

As we end our chat, we automatically mention a friend we have in common who left his earthly home in 2015 after a long life. In front of the American TV cameras, we talk briefly about the virtuous figure of Father Arturo Paoli, whom I mentioned earlier. He was an invaluable spiritual guide initially for Laura and Marco and then for Veronica and me. Smiling, we quote the verb that he invented and often used: *amorizzare*, roughly translated as "spreading love."

"We must spread love throughout the world," Arturo would always say. "When you go to the theater before the show begins, there is this great cacophony of noise from the musical instruments. Then, when the conductor arrives, it all becomes harmony, song, and beauty. In this way, we must turn discord into harmony by following our conductor, Jesus. Trusting in him, letting him lead us by the hand, asking his advice. Life is beautiful. It is we who make it ugly, sad, and agitated because we are dominated by this negative root that lies within us and which separates our positive qualities, which separates thought from love. We must unite them, create harmony and peace between reason and the heart."

I remember my first encounter with Father Arturo, theologian, writer, missionary, and tireless teacher of so many young people (one of the thousands of children he helped educate was Umberto Eco, who became an Italian writer and literary critic). When I turned up in front of him with my two older children, he immediately greeted me with great warmth but clearly had no idea who I was. This is partly why we got along right from the start. A friendship was born. On many occasions, Veronica and I sought solace in the reflections of this elderly missionary, finding new strength on our journey of faith.

Anyone who came to the clergy house of the community that he himself founded on the hills of Lucchesia would find a chair to rest on, a plate of warm food to satisfy their hunger, and Father Arturo's simple and powerful words to pacify their soul.

"It is God who chooses us. It is God who loves us," he would say. "Our duty is to look, be ready to be found, wait for him to reveal himself. No one knows how many ways God's will manifests itself on Earth! For me, looking for his kingdom means creating a more human, just, fraternal society. I am convinced that you do not necessarily need to be part of a church. The desire to believe is already an act of faith. Those who look are not atheists. What is my idea of God? The more you grasp his presence, the less you need to know who he is and where he is. What I feel is that God is spirit, the spirit that animates my life."

San Gimignano

The stretch of the journey to San Gimignano is charming but complicated. Our path is full of trees and branches being pushed out by the season to gain space and invade the narrow roads we travel along. We go past small villages such as Strove and Quartaia, as far as Campiglia, where the horses can rest. Our companion for a stretch of the journey is a young Texan musician and solo singer, Tauren Wells, the former front man of Royal Tailor, a Christian pop rock band. Also active in coaching and business activities, he and his wife, Lorna, have founded numerous music schools in the Houston area. Though he hails from the "land of horses," today is his first time on the back of a horse. He manages just fine.

Tauren tells us he has read about the immense sensitivity of horses, their ability to perceive their riders' mood, their fears, and the quality of their energy. Veronica suggests it is like an audience for a performing artist. The people can immediately grasp the artist's mood along with their intellectual integrity. You can never lie in front of an audience, nor should you.

Our Texan companion nods and tells us about his own experience. Many times, he has felt that God uses the songs he writes and performs to respond to what he himself is feeling and to remind him how he should not just think about his own problems and fears. "In reality, our singing does not stem from what we feel or express our feelings, but rather gives voice to faith and the responses of God," he says.

Taya Smith, a young singer from New South Wales, also rides with us for a few miles. She, too, will participate in our musical event at San Gimignano Cathedral. We promise to go visit her in Australia someday and ride along the magnificent beaches of her immense country. We finally reach the "Town of the Fine Towers," the "Medieval Manhattan," along the route followed by the Archbishop of Canterbury in the tenth century. After receiving a blessing in Piazza della Cisterna, we get ready to play music at the Collegiata di Santa Maria Assunta, San Gimignano's cathedral, a masterpiece of Tuscan Gothic architecture.

Under its three naves and within its fully frescoed walls, we sing before the TBN TV cameras as the sun cuts through the windows. The benches have been moved aside to make room for a grand piano in the center of the church. Here, we alternate between duets and solo performances. I am particularly pleased to sing "You'll Never Walk Alone" once more, together with Tauren and Taya, a reprise of the performance in San Galgano. Here, in the cathedral of San Gimignano, there is an extra special reason to perform it. My mother, Edi, is there. Though worn out by her failing health, she wanted to be here to listen to her son sing once more.

Mamma Edi

The trip to San Gimignano was one of her last. Now, as I write these notes and remember this experience, I think of my mother's great journey in life that has since ended. She was a generous, intelligent, hyperactive, competent, obstinate woman who was always ready to help others, a charismatic, beloved, respected character. Only those who had the chance to meet her in her prime can understand her greatness. In recent years, her many illnesses gradually emptied her precious essence.

When I was young, and it seemed that no one wanted to take a gamble on my talent, I remember that my mother went to Rome, unbeknownst to me, to talk in person with the stars of television entertainment at that time, stationing herself outside their houses to catch them and give them tapes of my singing. She contacted many private radio stations, distributing my first recorded songs and my first self-produced records. She always believed in me. She was always by my side and always helped me. For years, she worried about how my future would turn out. She even worked fifteen-hour days when she was younger with this in mind.

It is hard to fill a void this immense. However, I know that my mother left a body that was only causing her suffering at that point. It would be selfish to keep trying to forcefully lengthen an existence that had reached its end. We are all pilgrims passing through this world. I believe we will meet again someday. In the meantime, I carry my mother in my heart.

"We set out on our pilgrimage; the memory of this journey will remain with us forever throughout the rest of this greatest pilgrimage of ours."
(Photo © Luca Rossetti)

With Veronia in Saint Peter's Square, the heart of Christianity, to meet the Holy Father. (Photo © Luca Rossetti)

With Veronica, Virginia and Laura Biancalani, the president of the Andrea Bocelli Foundation. (Photo © Luca Rossetti)

Riding Caudillo. (Photo © Luca Rossetti)

Before Michelangelo's Pietà in Saint Peter's Basilica at the Vatican.
(Photo © Luca Rossetti)

Crossing the Aelian Bridge on horseback; also known as "Hadrian's bridge" after the Roman emperor who had it built in 134 AD. (Photo © Luca Rossetti)

The urban landscape began to thin out, making way for the countryside. The journey was now truly under way. (Photo © Luca Rossetti)

"The most beautiful music makes no sound. It is the peaceful, appreciative silence of a soul that meditates and presents itself before the eternal with wonder and serenity." (Photo © Luca Rossetti)

Inside the Santa Maria Assunta co-cathedral in Sutri. (Photo © Luca Rossetti)

With the soprano Clara Barbier at the ancient Roman amphitheater in Sutri. (Photo © Luca Rossetti)

(Photo © Luca Rossetti)

"We ride along white roads free of branches and scattered with handy springs where we stop every now and then to let our horses drink."
(Photo © Luca Rossetti)

Lake Bolsena, *"a peaceful body of water which formed three-hundred thousand years ago, a watery ring rimmed by low, sandy shores and surrounded by fields, vineyards, vegetable gardens and olive groves."* (Photo © Luca Rossetti)

Arriving at the Vitorchiano Trappist Monastery. (Photo © Luca Rossetti)

Singing Schubert's Ave Maria *together with the Trappist nuns.* (Photo © Luca Rossetti)

"Visiting Santa Cristina Basilica in Bolsena is one of the most moving moments of the entire pilgrimage." (Photo © Luca Rossetti)

"I am particularly delighted to have Virginia alongside me [...]. Thousands of years of life and history, the church contains the mortal remains of Saint Christina of Bolsena, the child saint. Veronica and I, alongside our daughter, pray together before her tomb." (Photo © Luca Rossetti)

On foot to Radicofani, towards the Medieval fortress. (Photo © Luca Rossetti)

Well-earned rest at the foot of Radicofani fortress, at the southern-most point of Val d'Orcia. (Photo © Luca Rossetti)

"'Sacred to nymphs and gods': this is how Bagno Vignoni is defined in an Ancient Roman inscription. [...] Piazza delle Sorgenti is truly magical with its enormous pool in the center framed by Renaissance buildings." (Photo © Luca Rossetti)

Matteo Bocelli reads his thoughts on the pilgrimage, in the cloister of Sant'Antimo Abbey. (Photo © Luca Rossetti)

In concert at Sant'Antimo Abbey, with the Teatro del Silenzio orchestra conducted by the maestro Beatrice Venezi. (Photo © Luca Rossetti)

Little setbacks mark the journey. (Photo © Lorenzo Montanelli)

Near San Quirico d'Orcia. (Photo © Luca Rossetti)

Among the thousand-year-old stones of Abbadia Isola (Monteriggioni) with two dear old friends: Laura Biancalani and the priest Marco Casalini. (Photo © Luca Rossetti)

"*I dedicate these days that I have narrated here to my mother, who is listening from Heaven, to Veronica, my partner in faith and in life, to my beloved children, to all my family, to my wider family at the Andrea Bocelli Foundation, and to all of you readers. You who are my brothers and sisters. My traveling companions.*" (Photo © Luca Rossetti)

CHAPTER 6

From San Gimignano to Lajatico

Toward Volterra

Just after we leave San Gimignano, there is an incident that could have turned into a tragedy. Two hundred miles into this pilgrimage, one of the horses is suddenly attracted to one of his traveling companions. We are riding downhill, and things seem to be going smoothly. But then this courser, who luckily has Emiliano at the reins, jumps on top of the horse in front. Its rider, Laurie from TBN, is completely unaware of the danger. It might have ended badly if not for the presence of mind and experience of our horse-keeper friend (who is also a former jockey, in showjumping, no less). All's well that ends well, but the entire group got a huge fright. There was a very high possibility that someone could have been badly hurt.

Little setbacks mark our journey, as is only to be expected. For instance, one time, Veronica said to me as we rode along: "You are right, you know. Giving me your horse was an excellent idea." I replied, "Yes, he is extremely reliable. He is afraid of tractors and cows, but that is it." With comical timing, barely a second later, Veronica turned to find herself face-to-face with an enormous cow. Her horse naturally became rattled and started flaring his nostrils. In this situation, the worst thing you can do is hesitate. My wife swiftly, and smoothly steered the horse past the potential obstacle. In the end, we laughed at our narrow escape.

We continue along and start to get the scent of home. We finally reach Volterra, the city of stone and alabaster, that translucent mineral that is skillfully sculpted here. The "city of wind" looks out over the valleys of the Cecina and Era rivers down below. This Etruscan town is truly unique with its tower houses and monuments. These include the thirteenth-century Palazzo dei Priori, the Romanesque cathedral, and the ruins of the Roman theater dating to the first century BC. Volterra's distinctiveness also stems from the fact that it was built on a drained sea (with its salt deposits), overlooking the cliffs of the famous Balze. These spectacular rock formations formed from the sandy, clay-like rock that would regularly collapse in ancient times, completely altering the geological structure and creating these characteristic sheer cliffs.

Volterra is especially dear to me. My firstborn son, Amos, was born in Volterra Hospital on February 22, 1995. I was at the Sanremo Musical Festival that day. I was performing a song that would, in a way, become a global classic, *Con te partirò*. Once my mother told me the wonderful news, I just had to get back to Volterra. I took my son in my arms and held him to my heart all night. Then, after just a few hours, I returned to Sanremo for the final song of the contest.

We let our horses rest. That evening, Veronica and I had the pleasure of having both Matteo and Amos by our sides. We have dinner together in a wonderful, lively atmosphere. Afterward, despite our weariness, we take the opportunity to "challenge each other" in our own way. Peacefully, in a noble, silent game.

The Sport of Thinking

On this occasion with Matteo and often with Amos and Virginia, we are always happy to spend some time on an activity that I particularly love, a way of spending time together and giving each other attention and focus.

I am referring to the game of chess, this fascinating sport of thinking. This strategic discipline has absorbed people from all over the world for over a millennium. It has chalked up striking aphorisms to describe it: a work of art between two minds, the art of war without carnage, a battle against errors, the supremacy of intelligence over force.

Chess has been my faithful pastime since I was a little boy. It was our family friend Aldo Ara who taught me the moves and the basics during a summer vacation on the Tuscan coast. I was so captivated by the game that it was not enough for me to just learn it. I wanted to understand it and study its subtleties by reading technical manuals. I still remember the manual written by Adriano Chicco and Giorgio Porreca. It included a description of a game played by the legendary chess player (and mathematician) Emanuel Lasker, which I learned by heart. It means victory in eight forced moves, which in technical jargon is called a "queen sacrifice," ending in checkmate with a castle.

These feats set my imagination alight! Back in the early seventies, even Italy caught word of the achievements of Bobby Fischer and Boris Spassky, world champions who helped popularize chess. Riding the wave of this excitement, I decided to build my own chessboard. I drew up a design. Using Formica wood, I made the black squares rough and the white squares smooth, getting a carpenter in Valdera to help me. The outcome was a very decent, resilient board. In fact, I still have it fifty years later.

Even as an adult, I have always happily accepted invitations to play a game. It is still a very enjoyable pastime, a great way to exercise and train the mind, and well recommended even for children. But chess is also an extraordinary metaphor for life. It is no coincidence that immense intellectuals, such as the philosopher Gottfried Leibniz and the great Leo Tolstoy, loved the game as a way of exercising their ability to think and loved the dynamics it evokes and triggers.

In my extremely limited experience, I am certain that playing chess has helped form my clear conviction that nothing in this world happens by chance and that luck has nothing to do with it in life, just as in chess.

Eros Ramazzotti

The curves of the hills become softer and more familiar. These are the final legs of our journey, our last encounters before arriving in Lajatico and the Teatro del Silenzio open-air amphitheater that lights up every summer under a ceiling of stars. To have large, strong wings, you need to have deep roots. My roots are here. I am the son of a farming culture and the values that have fortified this countryside for centuries. A house is a physical place. But the domestic aspect is tied to the affection that creates the emotional value. Home is experiencing the warmth, comfort, and joy of being with your family and sensing, with an inner smile, the greatest future peace of our heavenly home.

A pilgrimage is a journey, and every journey is made up of roads to be chosen and junctions to be faced. It is a powerful metaphor for life. At the root of every decision and every choice, you are faced with a crossroads. If you really dig deep, you will discover that the answers we seek lie at the roots of our conscience. And the right answer is the one that leads to good.

I am reminded of the words spoken by Pope Francis some years ago to people setting out on the Macerata to Loreto pilgrimage: "Pilgrimage is a symbol of life. It makes us think of life as walking. A soul that does not walk in life doing good is a soul that finishes in mediocrity and in spiritual poverty. Please do not stand still in life!"

For our final miles, Veronica, Emiliano Cioni, Pasquale Beretta, and I are joined by another dear friend, a well-known and beloved singer whom I have known for a quarter of a century: Eros Ramazzotti. As he is a good horseman and loves galloping, we ride some stretches at great speed. Then we slow down to enjoy the pleasure of chatting while riding along on our steeds.

Eros and I are both surprised to realize how few chances we have had to discuss spirituality over the years. Especially since we understand this aspect of life is extremely important to both of us. I tell him how I had decided to embark on this pilgrimage to "create silence" within me and listen more carefully to my spirit.

Even decades ago, though with the hesitant, disheveled means of youth, when traveling through this countryside, I had sensed what is much clearer to me today. The most beautiful music makes no sound. It is the peaceful, appreciative silence of a soul that meditates and presents itself before the eternal with wonder and serenity. Indeed, the sacred catalog that I propose is an auditory journey that aspires to silence. I hope it can stimulate the listener's desire to hear the music from a completely different source. The immortal music of the soul does not need notes. We carry it within us. We talk about faith and miracles, how they happen every day, without the media daring to report them, as they are so engrossed in broadcasting the world's disasters.

Time flies by. We are already coming up to Lajatico and its open-air theater. The theater is deserted right now, but one summer's evening every year it is filled with twelve thousand people from all over the world, from California to New Zealand, an audience that speaks different languages but is happy and fraternally connected by this miraculous union of nature and music.

Lajatico is my *buen retiro*, my native village, the place where my ancestors chose to live, work, and rear their children. It is still one of my favorite places to seek refuge whenever my work schedule allows it. I had to move to the countryside near the sea in Versilia in the second half of the nineties due to my allergy to grass plants, but I am still a child of these hills.

A Theater Named After Silence

It seemed like a crazy gamble at the start. I remember when my brother Alberto and our fellow Lajatico native Alberto Bartalini (both architects) each suggested the idea to me just a few hours apart. I initially believed it was simply unfeasible. After some hesitation and a night of reflection, I embraced the project with conviction, understanding that it could become a spectacular homage to the area.

The idea to use that natural bowl of extraordinary beauty among the hills surrounding Lajatico was intriguing, transforming it into a theater under the condition that it would immediately afterward be returned to the rustic landscape. The project was initially planned to last five years. But all the positive feedback we received made us decide to continue, partly not to waste what had become a resource in the meantime, with its significant spin-off effects on tourism in Valdera.

As I was saying earlier, silence is a formidable tool for creating space within us, space to reflect, listen, and learn. I named my autobiography in the late nineties after silence. I wrote it when I felt the need to go back over my life to better understand its meaning and perhaps to learn something in the process. I also decided to name this unique theater space after silence. Sitting there, immersed in the peace of the rolling hills, farmed fields, vines, and olive trees, its landscape is divided up into small plots, among the Cabernet, Sangiovese, and Merlot vineyards, among the scent of the cherries of Lari and the truffles of Volterra, among the aromas of the Mediterranean scrub.

The theater was built where peace and nature reign in a green and gray land dominated by the scent of hay, invaded in spring by clover and white primrose. Thousands of seats are placed on the terraced land here just once a year. Different musical friends of ours from all over the world are invited to perform at the annual concert. These have included Plácido

Domingo, Zubin Mehta, José Carreras, Roberto Bolle, Zucchero, Nicola Piovani, Pino Daniele, Riccardo Cocciante, Laura Pausini, Lang Lang, Sarah Brightman, David Foster, Lindsay Kemp, and Carla Fracci. Dozens and dozens of leading stars have come to Valdera and breathed in its atmosphere, celebrating the location with their talent.

Every year, a work of art is donated by an internationally acclaimed contemporary artist and placed at the back of the stage on the shores of a small man-made lake. Works by Arnaldo Pomodoro, Hans Peter Ditzler, Kurt Laurenz Metzler, Giuseppe Carta, and Park Eun Sun have become the symbol and scenery of every single edition.

The entire area has an ancient beauty. It is a welcoming land far from the din of modern life. We ride the horses around the lake up to the stage of the Teatro del Silenzio. We proceed around the perimeter (circling around the monumental sculpture *Clio Dorada* by Manolo Valdés in the center, an enigmatic protagonist in golden brass and stainless steel), where we would return a few hours later for the final musical event of our pilgrimage.

Borgo Natio (*My Native Village*)

After riding up to the Teatro del Silenzio with Eros, we stop off in the village for a coffee at our friend Daniele's bar. Then we leave Lajatico and head out toward La Sterza to reach the small cemetery there.

My pilgrimage would lack a sense of completion without this last stop, without paying homage to the memory of my father, who rests here. When my father passed away, I remember having the unmistakable feeling that there was not even one atom of him left in his body. We are what is inside this earthly guise. Once we leave it, we go elsewhere, where I will join my father and embrace him again.

Twenty years have passed, but the melancholy generated by his absence has never abated. It has not been remedied by time (which you would think should soften the edges and heal the wounds). This is why I wanted to come here today and take some time to pray.

The farther afield my work has taken me, the more I have felt the urge to return to these hills. I want to offer something deeply intimate and personal to our American friends from the network documenting the pilgrimage that is now nearing its end, so I decided to share a little literary homage, a poem, *Borgo natio* ("My Native Village"), that I wrote a dozen years ago in Copenhagen, dedicated to the village where I was born. This is my way of expressing my gratitude to this land and its people, to my family, to my fellow natives living here today, and to all those who have spent and ended their earthly journey here with their ups and downs, their stories, and their loves.

Hoping that my emotions do not get the better of me and choke up my voice, I cite the verses in front of the US TV cameras, thinking of my father and all my loved ones.

> *Piccola terra dei miei primi passi*
> *Delle mie prime lacrime innocenti,*
> *almeno, quei momenti ritrovassi,*
> *di gioie passeggere, di tormenti*

senza ragione: fole di fanciullo,
che spera, che dispera e guarda avanti,
piccola Arcadia, ancora in te m'annullo;
in te mi perdo, mi ritrovo e quanti

come me t'hanno amato e sono andati,
dell'opra loro a te, lasciando traccia,
seco, portando il verde dei tuoi prati,
l'odore di maggesi e di vinaccia.

E quanti, t'hanno cantato, tutti in coro,
col loro accento schietto e melodioso!
Quante braccia sfinite dal lavoro
di te hanno fatto quel bene prezioso

che io custodirò gelosamente
conchiuso nel mio cuore innamorato
di ciò che in te dimora, della gente,
degli ubertosi clivi che ho mirato!

E non m'attosca il tempo ch'è passato,
l'idea fosca di quello che mi resta,
anzi, giova al cuor mio disincantato,
l'incanto di quei luoghi ornati a festa,

or dal risveglio della primavera,
or dal vitreo candore dell'inverno,
tu, selvaggia m'appari, ma sincera,
mia dolce terra! Paradiso eterno

di pace, di ricordi, tanto cari,
che tremo nel cercare le parole,
piccole, inadeguate, come fari,
a rischiarar ciò, che già ride al sole.

Il tuo sole che là, tra quei cipressi,
scalda memorie e lacrime cocenti,
abbracci senza fine, eterni amplessi,
ci doni ancora i suoi tramonti ardenti.[1]

Food for the Soul

Some have defined poetry as a love letter to the world, some an act of peace, others the art of getting the sea to fit into a glass. The point is poetry is necessary. The heart, spirit, and inner voice of everyone needs to be nourished.

The world needs poetry. We need sources of inspiration, friendly voices, teachers, and support that take us by the hand and lead us through the world of spirituality. We desperately need this to find the right path, to better understand our feelings, to accept our defeats, and to find the energy to pursue our aspirations.

This is why I have always encouraged my children to consider the act of reading poetry, internalizing verses, as a secret tonic, a vitamin for the soul. I have also urged them not to be ashamed of their own poetry and to put their thoughts and loves down on paper. The goal is for each of us to make our lives a long poem.

"He who sings prays twice"—the words of Saint Augustine. Writing poetry, I venture to say, is also a bit like praying because prayer is the act of addressing the sacred dimension through words. Those who write poetry question their inner depths, tuning into a higher dimension. As with prayer, poetry requires humility as well as inspiration and sensitivity. It requires the tenacity to bend to its rules and form.

My modest poetic feats express a space where I have gathered my sincerest feelings. They act like a laboratory, a training ground where I have challenged myself with the limits imposed by metrics.

In the introduction to a small volume of my poems, I wrote: "To those who would ask where to find me, without hesitation, I would say: 'In my humble verses.' Do not look for anything else, despite their paucity. It is there you can find my fervent, unending pursuit of beauty, inconsistencies, the need for air, space, freedom, for the music that hides between words, for kindness, for life, and faith. At the fringes of reality, I have searched. I will continue to ceaselessly search for the point of convergence between what is beautiful and what is good, firm in my belief that everything beautiful is good and vice versa."

Poggioncino

Traveling the last hundred feet toward our farm at Poggioncino triggers turmoil within me. Its aromas are like a time machine, an extremely powerful vehicle that whips up complex scenes and strong emotions. My mind goes to the smell of hay and the smell of the earth after a summer downpour. I think of the celebration of the harvest, the old-style harvest, reaping wheat, and building haystacks. I think of the beloved road that I have traveled down thousands of times and that we are now galloping down. The road to home: I know it like the back of my hand.

We slow down. Veronica and I take each other by the hand. We are home. I would like to say to her: None of this would have been possible without you. I would like to say this to Emiliano, Pasquale, the directors Paolo and Gaetano, and all my traveling companions.

But there is no time. Once we get past the gate, we are surprised by a crowd of friends and family waiting for us in the garden. It is 5:15 p.m. on Saturday, May 22, 2021. Applause and joyous greetings welcome our arrival. I joke about how Rome truly is far away. I call out to my son Matteo and hand him the reins as I dismount my horse. A physical but also metaphorical handover. There is a wonderfully joyous atmosphere. In addition to the strong affection of so many people, I can sense their desire and indisputable need to come together to get back to socializing after so many restrictions during the most severe phases of the pandemic.

We bring everyone to the huge round table that stands beside the ornamental garden. There, we sing, we celebrate, and we drink to each other's health. I play the guitar and then pass it to Eros, who generously plays us one of his songs. A drone flies over the property, so we gather together in the center of the yard as it films us.

The farm at Poggioncino is mainly there for the horse stables. But for me, it is the finest house there is. It meets the key qualities of being livable, transmitting serenity, and welcoming all those who enter it. It has been ours for generations. Formerly the lodgings of the family's farm, it underwent a complex restyling some years ago by my brother Alberto. It also exhibits the artistic touch of Alberto Bartalini, our friend and partner since way back.

I would always yearn to see my animal friends here when I came as a child with my mother and father. When I was around thirty, I came to live here by myself. After I got my law degree, when I had stepped up my piano bar sessions to support myself financially, I spent unforgettable nights and days in Poggioncino. Though I have now given up that libertine side of my youthful escapades, still today, I feel the joy and happiness of friendship, the warmth of evenings spent entertaining. The long table in the kitchen embodies this spirit. It seats up to twenty people and conjures up the pleasure of dining in company.

When the weather prevents me from going out on my horse, I love studying and playing music here in Poggincino. Just as my homes in Forte dei Marmi and Miami, there is no lack of musical instruments here. We often meet up here with the Andrea Bocelli Foundation team and volunteers to plan, design, celebrate, and enjoy each other's company.

Katherine Jenkins

Up to now, the pilgrimage's musical settings have been churches and theaters, masterpieces designed by human genius. In this final stage, the architect is God himself, and the backdrop is nature, his greatest masterpiece.

We sing, once again, to celebrate this journey through the hills and valleys of Lazio and Tuscany along the paths of our souls. We place our musical instruments and music stands on the turf of the Teatro del Silenzio. Our friend Beatrice Venezi directs the orchestra one more time. We also have the cello player Hauser with us once again. By my side is another friend and fellow singer, Katherine Jenkins, a Welsh mezzo-soprano who sang on this very special stage in 2009 along with Plácido Domingo, Toquinho, and others.

We use the songs to express what we could not say solely with words: "I Believe," "Amazing Grace," "Inno Sussurrato" (Whispered Hymn), and "The Lord's Prayer." We pray by singing. With all my heart, I thank God and all my traveling companions, all the people I met along the way, all the emotions I felt, all the things that happened, both happy events and setbacks, and all the moments I experienced.

The end of our journey is always the start of a journey for someone else. There is nothing more joyful than seeing this as a member of the US production staff, Kristian Kelly, proposes to his coworker on stage. He goes down on one knee before her, offers her a ring, and asks her to marry him, to testify before God this wonderful and courageous decision to create a new family.

The stall area is still sloping ground covered in grass and will remain so until July. Last year, for the first time in fifteen years, we could not have an audience due to the pandemic. We organized a great show despite this in 2020. It was dedicated to hope and broadcast via streaming. Instead of people, we filled the stalls with thousands of flags from all over the world.

"Of Liberty He Journeys"

I wrote this at the start of this story, and I want to get back to it now at the end of the story. Part of the impetus that triggered the whole adventure—together with our strong spiritual motivations—is linked to freedom: a value, an inalienable right, put to the test in recent years during the public health emergency that assailed the planet.

"Of liberty, he journeys: that how dear. They know, who for her sake have life refus'd," wrote Dante Alighieri in Purgatory Canto 1 of his Divine Comedy. This is a right for which many have fought and died. I humbly offer my experience here without judgment and without solutions to pull out of my hat. I always uphold the belief that you should never willingly relinquish your freedom for any reason whatsoever, even if it seems a most noble reason. No one has the right to alienate your freedom.

So many times, in the most far-flung places on the planet, I have yearned with all my being for the tranquility and serenity of my home, the company of my children, the silence, the calm of my bedroom, the joyous greeting of my dogs. I feel this even more strongly when my poor nerves are frayed with the strain of long journeys, the numerous appointments, the tension of so many performances, always in the spotlight and always exposed to the severe judgment of the audience and the critics. Many times, I have begun to count down the days and even hours to that moment when I would cross the threshold of my home and breathe in that dear familiar smell.

That dream came true, alas, in one of the most tragic periods the world has experienced since World War II. On a sad evening in March 2020, my country, shaken and stunned by an unexpected and unprecedented epidemic, received the mandatory order broadcast on all television networks to stop all working activities and stay locked up at home until further notice.

From that moment, we found ourselves imprisoned in our own homes, though innocent of any crime. So, the dream I had cultivated for months, for years, a forbidden, impossible dream, suddenly became a reality, but unfortunately, in the guise of a nightmare. After that, on March 10, I remained in my lovely home in Forte dei Marmi for months, in perfect harmony with my loved ones, with my closest collaborators, and with my dogs. Outside, the sun shone while the road down to the sea was deserted. Nothing disturbed that peace I had been craving forever. The birds were singing happily, and the sky was clear. In the absence of traffic, the air was clean and fragrant with the scents of spring. Everything seemed to be people-friendly again in a long-forgotten way.

Over those weeks, in that silence, I clearly remember the sound of a voice penetrating deep into my heart, getting louder and more persistent every day. "Have you forgotten me?" it seemed to chastise me. "Do you not know that I have been with you since the day you came into the world and that you will crave me until your last breath? Do you not know, or do you not remember, that I am your most important gift from the heaven that created you? Why do you not look for me? Why do you not defend me? Do you not need me anymore? Have you perhaps forgotten my name? I am freedom. Without me, everything you love and everything that is objectively beautiful and pure and desirable, all of that is lost in the void left by my absence. Do love and freedom not always go hand in hand? And is it, not love and freedom that generate what is legitimately called happiness?"

Man is born free and has the right to die free. It is in the holy concept of freedom that we find the mystery of life, awareness, and joy, a mystery that lies in every human condition.

In Cammino
(On the Road)

I want to give special thanks to you, reader, for your goodwill and patience in staying with me this far. The hope of making a modest contribution in sharing my values was what spurred me to turn my hand to writing, this discipline that I respect and dedicate time to, but always as an amateur. However, urged on by my publisher and various friends, I accepted the challenge of putting into writing this long journey on horseback. By writing about the pilgrimage, I have had the chance to relive it with intensity, reviving the emotions and reflections that sprouted along the way.

More than a year has now passed since our journey. In the meantime, while the world has been struggling to drag itself out of the grief of the pandemic and the ensuing deep societal and psychological wounds, a new scourge has struck the world; a war in Ukraine, another conflict to add to the many that have already inflamed our wretched planet.

I remain optimistic. In fact, I now feel an even stronger desire and will to speak to the hearts of people and continue to tirelessly create, spread, and encourage beauty. Every war is the opposite of beauty; that goes without saying. There are no winners in war.

The days go by, and with every rising of the sun, life gives us another portion of our earthly pilgrimage. Instead of mounting my steed, however, I travel by airplane to meet those who are kind enough to appreciate my music, wherever they may be in the world. The best way to thank them is to do so in person through my live performances, so I intend to continue to do that as long as God allows.

After my thirty years in this profession, music is my remedy and my way of instilling levity, hope, and positivity into life.

I recently had the unexpected joy of singing and recording a Christmas album together with two of my children, Matteo and Virginia. This in itself was a bonus gift that life had in store for me. But it will be even better if our voices can spark a moment of reflection or a smile in listeners, one of those disarming and encouraging smiles we used to have when we were children.

All over the world, art and culture are a tool of shared awareness and support for development and peace between peoples. They help people come together and put aside their mistrust of one another. I am reminded of a motto I wrote many years ago: "When art is life, it is art. When life is art, it is life". Culture (and thus art) is a gift from heaven to help nurture our spirit. If we do not nurture our spirit, it might regress. Without culture, without art, nothing can be truly resolved.

I dedicate these days that I have narrated here to my mother, who is listening from heaven; to Veronica, my partner in faith and in life; to my beloved children; to all my family; to my wider family at the Andrea Bocelli Foundation; and to you and all other readers. You are my brothers and sisters, my traveling companions.

Meditation

Fire doesn't generate life; it destroys it. It cannot thrive in the harsh, freezing conditions of absolute zero. Fire and ice—this is the scene at the universe's origin where life appeared as if by magic. What role can chance have played in this mysterious event?

Chance is capable of anything in the field of great numbers, but it is helpless against the power of the impossible. The most improbable combination of numbers or letters is always possible, but it needs numbers or letters. Basically, it needs the essential conditions; otherwise, the combination remains a mere abstract concept.

At the origin of the universe, fire, and ice show up as elements that make the birth and development of any kind of life form irrefutably absurd.

Then again, five or six light chimes at regular intervals are enough to convince us of the presence of a clock, or at least a mechanism, created by human genius in order to accurately measure time.

In every block of pure white marble lies a multitude of inanimate bodies, ready to step into the light of the sun and the judgment of people, an infinite number of ideas in the prison of the material, ready to be freed by the sharp, skilled strikes of the chisel of an inspired artist. Every block hides a Pietà, but only the genius of Michelangelo has gifted one to all of humanity.

Who would be willing to believe in the genius of chance before a work like that?

Who but a madman would be willing to attribute to the bizarre designs of chance the building of a splendid basilica, a lavish palace, or even a plain rural hut? Yet, there are people who do not hesitate to attribute to chance the less fortuitous, the most unique and divine of architectures, the most evident of intelligent and wonderfully intelligible volition that, for good reason, we call *creation*.

Evolved spirits and bright minds who desperately deny the evidence of human intellectual sparsity attribute to change everything that they cannot understand and reasonably explain. However, they instinctively believe that not even chance could generate a human creature in a mother's womb without the necessary and indispensable act of conception. Atheists always find it easier to laugh at those with faith rather than refute a dogma using the concepts they use to explain reason over everything in existence.

So much proud naivety and so much pitiful affectation is rampant among humans, especially when they venture to grope blindly through the field of faith! At the foundation of this reasoning, there is a plain and simple choice to be made, a crossroads where your way of thinking must choose which direction to take: the path of chance or the path that leads toward God.

When a person opts for chance, then everything that has anything to do with the basis of religion becomes undoubtedly useless, if not ridiculous. Even talking about it is an unforgivable waste of precious time. There are many highly educated people in positions of great responsibility, rational people who are usually commendably inclined to doubt their own opinions and yet who do not hesitate, whenever they get a chance, to laugh at or shout out rashly against the dogmas of faith, such as the Immaculate Conception.

Their loud, powerful tone is striking and disconcerting, as is the arrogance of their discourse against the sacrament of confession. "So," they say, "a person with several university degrees, with unrivaled life experience, who is honest and capable, charismatic even, should kneel at the feet of some little country priest, barely literate, pompous and horrifyingly obscene, and start telling him their business and repent with acts of submission!"

Are there not rules descending directly from natural law that dictate absolute and unconditional respect for our fathers, even the worst of them, as inept, drunk, violent, or simply closed-minded as they may be? And could God not have good reason, incomprehensible to man, to ask his children the to have intellectual humility to genuflect before an authority put there by God himself? If nothing else, but to teach them to grow in the most important human virtue: humility.

Those who opt for chance as the solution to all problems, even existential issues, end up seeing the God on which everything depends in the concept of chance. Meanwhile, in courthouses all over the world, people are frequently denied credence and are condemned as they desperately attempt to show the pure and simple bad luck of facts. Facts that are ostensibly random and only vague, as well as very improbable, due to the volition of humans. The numerous innocents languishing in the world's prisons know this all too well—powerless, unsuspecting victims of the strange coincidences that the judge refused to recognize when evaluating their case.

But this seeming triumph of reason implicates the death of the spirit. A person raising chance above the altar of God is like someone preferring to move in the dark rather than in the warm, reassuring light of the sun. The light of his own intellect will help him like a match struck in the darkness of a stormy night.

How can people hope to understand God using their intellectual faculties? There is not enough room in the human mind to imagine the infinity of elements required to access such a high degree of consciousness. It would be as if a computer or a robot tried to understand humans, that is, its creator.

Those who deify chance are not without a god, but they settle for a deity who rolls the dice and who cannot be asked or blamed for anything. Meanwhile, those who look for God, who truly look for him by way of their heart, which is the only way that leads to the destination, find him without fail. They overcome despair and proceed with hope, the first precious gift from God to the pure in heart, to the simple, to the poor in spirit, who, to be clear, are not foolish, inept, or incapable but instead are wise. I'm speaking of those who let themselves be won over by the allure of creation, the enchantment of nature, and respect it. Perhaps they study creation and delve into it to find within it the most profound reasons to love the God who created it all.

But the search for truth is a concentric path with no short-cuts. It requires method, patience, perseverance, and a strong desire to reach the finish line. We reach for truth when nothing is expected. We merely hope to edge closer to it someday. That is our keen desire.

The path to truth does not require any particular kind of superior intelligence. Human intelligence is an eye that sees the path already completed, the problems of this life, earthly matters, in the spaces reserved for knowledge. Intelligence looks backward. It cannot see ahead. The pure of heart, the poor in spirit, the simple, the humble, these are the people who advance, instinctively, toward the truth. It attracts them as a powerful magnet attracts iron.

Bewitched by worldly seductions, all of the rest remorselessly criticize the love, pain, and passions that dramatically shake up the idea of the coincidence of life—life that they should attribute to him, which encompasses all the divine attributes of the eternal and infinite. Or do some intend to refute the eternity of time and the infinity of space, imagining a bell tolling at the end of time and a giant wall at the edge of the universe? Even our poor minds, floundering in these seas, knowing little or nothing of it all, understand that these seas exist, and we are part of them.

If that is true, what value has the fleeting pain that lasts a second, an hour, or a year compared to eternal happiness? Or, conversely, what value has the fleeting joy and pleasure that lasts a second compared to eternal torment?

Less, I believe, much less value than a child attributes to the cruelest punishment or the most desired toy. Yet, people often ask why we have adversities, illnesses, old age with its tribulations, early deaths, and all the suffering of this world. Just as children ask why they have so much homework, so many rules imposed by parents, and so many severe punishments, all of these things they will understand the meaning and value of later on. One day, they will even long for those times, those parents, those strict teachers, affectionately remembering those trifling vexations that made such an enormous contribution to forming their character.

God's logic is incomprehensible to us to the point that it even seems adversarial at times. How could that not be so? Maybe we do not need this life. We could do without it, like a child could do without school or a family. Like an athlete could do without training or a sick person could do without a hospital.

Like good students, those who hope for a merciful God know that reward does not come without effort, without sacrifice, and without tribulations. So, they immediately give their best, no matter the cost, in order to earn the compassion of he who represents the only way of salvation, the only escape from the horrors and deceptive flattery of this world.

Those who place their fate in chance, aware that they are inevitably advancing toward the end of their days on earth, will find it hard to resist the temptation to engage in everything that turns to their advantage, indifferent to the risk of causing pain and despair to their neighbor, indifferent to the most terrible risk of finding themselves, sooner or later, in front of he who deals out eternal life or punishment. But the advantages are the illusory pleasures that last a second until anxiety, dissatisfaction, and loss take the reins. And so on, relentlessly, until the end—a terrible, shocking end without solace.

This is how the path of faith offers humankind an irrefutably advantageous gamble, very much like that of a hard-working student who listens carefully to the voice of their conscience, uncomfortable as it may be, and decides to apply themselves with all their energy, willingly accepting the sacrifice, ordeals, competition with their companions, struggles of exams, strict teachers, and everything that good schooling entails. All in the hope of deserving, in the end, a life full of honest satisfaction and the respect of their acquaintances, work colleagues, and superiors.

So, faith is like a unique win-win wager. If you win, you win everything; if you lose, you lose nothing, nothing that is worth saving. You are wagering with money that can already be considered out of the running, and the investment can pay out a treasure of incalculable value. The old saying "There's no harm in trying" doesn't quite cover it. "There is harm in not trying" sounds much more appropriate. If we examine it closely, denying the existence of God is infinitely more absurd than denying the existence of the clockmaker who patiently created and assembled the pieces of our clock, or the builder who constructed the house that protects us from the weather, or the engineer who designed the speeding car that disappears over the horizon in a split second, or Michelangelo who sculpted the *Pietà*.

An atheist is like an orphan who, asked where they came from, replies: "My mother and father? They don't exist. I have never met them. I have never heard anything about them. I don't know what they look like or what they sound like. I was found in a dumpster where I materialized by chance one day. Therefore, I am a child of chance."

On the other hand, there are people who have never met their parents, who don't know where they are or if they are even still alive, but none of them, not even in these particularly unfortunate cases, considers themselves a child of chance.

An atheist is like someone who wakes up in the morning and finds a steaming cup of tea on their bedside table; rather than simply wondering who was so kind to have left that cup of tea there for them, instead wonders how it just materialized there beside their bed. No one would ever believe it was a matter of chance, even if they failed to discover who had come into their room while they were sleeping and then left again, leaving that act of generosity as the only clue.

Apart from that, so many things elude the capacities of our mediocre senses. Radio waves exist, though our ears cannot hear them. Microorganisms exist, though our eyes cannot see them, and our hands cannot touch them. How many elements are there that people do not know or cannot explain that elude the control and judgment of the human mind—the human mind that then deigns to explain the origin of the universe using its paltry faculties?

Chained up in the prison of its body, distressed and confused by the laws of this world, the human being finds itself desperately searching for the meaning of life and, as a result, searching for a purpose, a goal, a direction. But, alas, the answers it seeks are beyond the limits of its intellect. It must have patience and perseverance. It must burn passionately for the truth, ready to work hard and pay any price to find it.

As scripture says, "seek and ye shall find" (Matthew 7:7 KJV). Those who seek, in this case, find for all eternity. They find happiness that never fades. Everyone's goal is to find happiness. Those who seek it with humility and through their heart also find the meaning and the first and sole purpose of human existence.

Searching for the Father and hoping to find him means fully committing yourself to a frenzied search for love. And love, as we know, defies the control of reason. Rather it mocks reason when reason believes it can dominate love, and it goes straight to the heart where the cry for help originates.

The newborn pilgrim taking their first steps on their earthly journey knows nothing of this world. They do not know their mother or father. They feel the need to feed, blindly seek their mother's breast, and quickly discover love, an overflowing, absolute love for the person who gave them life, who envelops them with care and warmth. Even before their vocal tract allows them to speak those first wonderful words, that little being loves. They love their mother and father, and they seek them; they trust them entirely and are happy. They love and are loved. Without knowing it, they are enveloped and protected by an immeasurable love that they experience obliviously.

Is a person's condition with the God who generated life and the universe so different? "He who has ears to hear, let him hear" (Mark 4:9).

As for those who do not want to hear, what can we say to them?

A person who believes themselves to be a child of chance experiences to varying degrees the anxiety of passing the time relentlessly leading toward old age, sickness, and death, yet imposes morals, judges, and passes sentences. Just like the God he insists on denying, dutifully obeying the cry of the species and his mysterious designs, he produces children, human beings who, in his vision of the world, are, like himself, wretched children of chance condemned to a life of tribulations, which sooner or later ends in the tragic event of death devoid of hope. Despite that, he trusts in their love, forgetting that he himself was behind their earthly drama.

What kind of arcane principle of logic or morals governs such behavior? It is very hard to fathom, just as it is difficult to understand how atheists manage to recruit others. While it is easy to explain the desire of those who wish to transmit their optimism to others, their faith in the future, and the hope that lights the way for each of us, there is something mysteriously sinister in the behavior of those who apply all their energy to spreading a vision of the world and of human life that eliminates everything good and beautiful that spontaneously blossoms in the heart of man.

Humans are fatefully called to choose between good and evil. They are free to act, think, judge, decide, build, or destroy. Free in everything but forced to choose between good and evil. How do we do this?

First and foremost, you need to decipher good and evil and remove their masks, cloaks, and layers formed by misinterpretations of the language. And then advance tenaciously toward the light.

The greatest good is happiness. Extreme evil is the opposite.

Those who hold hope in their heart are happy. Those who lose hope fall into despair, the worst of all evils. As a result, it is easy to conclude that those who sow hope do good, while those who sow despair do evil. Those who inspire others to have faith create lasting hope, hope that makes people happy. Those who inspire others to atheism take away hope, thus generating despair and unhappiness.

Life is a clear and indisputable fact. The wish to find the Father, the Creator, is natural and just. Assuming his nonexistence from the start means giving up on attributing clear meaning to life, reducing this wonderful mystery to a sad and improbable, or probably impossible, chance event between primordial elements existing in the abyss of the void without reason, without explanation, by no one's volition.

Imprisoned within the insurmountable confines of time and space, man is like a little chick waiting inside an egg for the moment to break through the shell and discover another world with completely different rules and dimensions. However, this little being, this insignificant speck of stardust, understands that there are no clocks without clockmakers, there are no engineering works without engineers, there is no effect without cause, there is no cause without law, there is no law without a legislator. That should be enough to drive you to choose hope, hope that quickly becomes a certainty through the ways of the heart that there would be no life without God.

Due to his very nature—fragile, changeable, inclined toward disobedience and betrayal—man now finds himself forced to live, as I said earlier, by choosing between good and evil at every turn. Between good, which is always a child of good, and evil, which is always and exclusively a child of evil. Between good, which is born and is a gift from love, and evil, which is the offshoot of hatred.

The purpose of good is to purify the human soul and give it the supreme gift of lost happiness. The purpose of evil, on the other hand, is to pollute the human soul, poison it, and cast it into doubt and then into despair.

The objectives of evil are naturally much easier to achieve because good is similar to evil as building is to destroying. At the same time, mistakes are to truth as the transient bliss of idleness is to the honest and lasting satisfaction of work.

Evil is a child of evil and the father of doubt. Not that healthy kind of doubt that feeds thought and causes all human certainty to waver, but rather that terrible kind of doubt that obscures the part of the human intellect that depends on the heart and allows man to be stupefied, to fall in love and to fall to his knees before the wonders of nature, of which he is part. Therefore, the purpose of evil is deadly doubt.

The purpose of evil is to whisper in the ear of man the false and poisonous idea: "I am here; therefore, there cannot be a God! Because if God existed and was truly omnipotent, he would not let me, evil, slither around among men, bearing blood and tears, pain and dismay."

The temptation to surrender to this reasoning is frighteningly strong because man's nature is tragically limited and weak. It is true that God allows evil, just as a good father allows a child to be scolded, truly punished, to experience severity, difficulty, and sacrifice so that he may grow stronger and become an upright, brave, and willing person. Yet a child does not doubt the love of their father, not even those who feel abandoned. So why should man doubt God's love when the troubles afflicting him have no explanation? Does God not have all of eternity to explain his logic and rules for governing the universe to his children?

God is like a precious book, hidden among thousands of other finely bound volumes that are painstakingly aligned to make the best impression but lack any depth or artistic value. The book is there, accessible, with its immense content, usefulness, clarity, and sincerity of intent. You just have to look for it. You just have to want to find it, want to read it, assimilate it. Plainly bound, it has no title on the cover nor any grandiose names. There are just a few pages, expressed with the simplicity of a child, written in a way that everyone can understand.

However, understanding those pages means understanding the will of God; it does not mean understanding God. Because God, in his greatness, is incomprehensible to man. It would be easier for the little chick inside the egg waiting to break out to understand how it was conceived and know its parents even before directly experiencing it. That would be easier than for man to comprehend the reasons and mechanisms of creation and know the God who created everything.

Nevertheless, atheists see believers as naive people who accept the fairy tale of a God creator and lord of heaven and earth. Believers see atheists as presumptuous egocentrics who see the world, the entire universe, as a complex machine that materialized out of nothing under the aegis of pure chaos. But while atheists would seriously doubt the sanity of someone who believed in the materialization of any random ordinary object, believers never doubt the existence of an artist when they find themselves admiring a work of genius, a work that always stems from an act of love.

So, God is love, speaks of love, and advises us to love. But what love does he speak of? What kind of love does he advise?

He who conceived and created the world asks us to love our enemies as our friends and love them even more! Is it possible that he who knows everything created man to ask something of us mortals that goes way beyond our natural human possibilities? Is it possible that God asks the impossible of us? Miracles are his prerogative, so humans cannot perform miracles, not even on themselves. They cannot turn hate into love, just as they cannot turn water into wine. So, what does the Maker mean when he asks us to love one another as he has loved us? (John 13:34.)

Like a good father, God loves everyone. Therefore, he places the good of others into our hands.

Though it may be impossible to love your enemies with the same love you feel for your friends, it is possible to act the same, with the same level of attention and using the same criteria, and to relate to your enemies as you do to your friends, with the certain knowledge that good always generates good, and vice versa.

How can you hope to win and divide the spoils of victory among the members of a team if the team is not united, if it is split by factions and fighting rather than cooperation? Life is a huge team game where we are all called to put aside any kind of personal hostility for the good of everyone and for our own good.

So, loving in the Christian sense means caring for your neighbor, be they friend or foe. The good that each individual does will swiftly generate more good at an incalculably higher quantity, which will wash over humanity in time and space beyond the imagination.

This kind of love is the shortest path to truth. It is the immediate solution to the most ancient problems. It is the theorem of all theorems, the cure for all ailments. Thus, loving means caring—caring for everyone at any cost.

In order to make this divine rule ours, we need to reflect deeply on what we are, on the talent that we unforgivably rush to claim as our own, on the presumed merits we attribute to ourselves with hasty carelessness, on the distinctive characteristics that pathetically boost our ego, dangerously undermining the roots of any possible spiritual development.

What part have we played in the creation of our features, of our incredible talent, of that charisma we treasure so dearly and show off to benefit from these strictly personal advantages? What have we done to obtain a rock-hard will, higher-than-average abilities, physical stamina, and even moral strength? What great things can we truly claim as our own that do not in fact derive from he who created the world and its rules?

If we at least had the intellectual strength to give an honest answer to these questions, it would be easier to take the first step on the path of love, that love that Christ demonstrated on the cross. Love: it will be easier to fully understand this tiny, immense word, so empty and yet so full of content, depending on the diligence, manner, and perspective we adopt, depending on the use we wish to make of it over our lifetime. And, as if by magic, we will all feel a bit closer, a bit more alike, a bit less alone, freer, and, above all, happier.

Andrea Bocelli

Endnote

1 *Borgo natio* ("My Native Village") English Translation

Oh, the land where I took my first steps
and spilled my first innocent tears;
if only I could return to those times
of fleeting joys, of groundless torments

Those times of a young boy
who hopes, despairs, and looks ahead,
oh little Arcadia, I lose myself in you,
in you, I disappear and find myself once more

How many like me have loved you and left,
leaving a trace of their labor with you,
taking with them the green of your meadows
and the scent of your fallow fields and musty marc

How many have sung your praises, in chorus,
with their plain and melodious voices!
How many tired working arms
have left a treasured memory

Which I will hold deep in my heart,
loving all that resides in you,
the people, and the bountiful hillsides
upon which I have gazed!

And I am not aggrieved by the time passed
The dark idea of what time remains
It gladdens my disenchanted heart to feel entranced
by those places decorated for celebration

Or to see the awakening of spring
Or the glassy candor of winter
You appear wild to me, and yet sincere
My sweet land, eternal paradise of peace

And of memories so dear
that I tremble searching for those small and inadequate words,
    like beacons,
to risk what already laughs in the sun.
Your sun, there among those cypress trees,
warms memories and tears together, endless embraces,
eternal joy, and still bestows on us its fiery sunsets.

Made in the USA
Monee, IL
27 September 2024

66472607R00105